HUMAN RIGHTS VETTING: NIGERIA AND BEYOND

HEARING

BEFORE THE

SUBCOMMITTEE ON AFRICA, GLOBAL HEALTH, GLOBAL HUMAN RIGHTS, AND INTERNATIONAL ORGANIZATIONS

OF THE

COMMITTEE ON FOREIGN AFFAIRS
HOUSE OF REPRESENTATIVES

ONE HUNDRED THIRTEENTH CONGRESS

SECOND SESSION

JULY 10, 2014

Serial No. 113–196

Printed for the use of the Committee on Foreign Affairs

Available via the World Wide Web: http://www.foreignaffairs.house.gov/ or http://www.gpo.gov/fdsys/

U.S. GOVERNMENT PRINTING OFFICE

88–627PDF   WASHINGTON : 2014

For sale by the Superintendent of Documents, U.S. Government Printing Office
Internet: bookstore.gpo.gov   Phone: toll free (866) 512–1800; DC area (202) 512–1800
Fax: (202) 512–2104   Mail: Stop IDCC, Washington, DC 20402–0001

COMMITTEE ON FOREIGN AFFAIRS

EDWARD R. ROYCE, California, *Chairman*

SUBCOMMITTEE ON AFRICA, GLOBAL HEALTH, GLOBAL HUMAN RIGHTS, AND INTERNATIONAL ORGANIZATIONS

CHRISTOPHER H. SMITH, New Jersey, *Chairman*

CONTENTS

HUMAN RIGHTS VETTING: NIGERIA AND BEYOND

THURSDAY, JULY 10, 2014

House of Representatives,
Subcommittee on Africa, Global Health,
Global Human Rights, and International Organizations,
Committee on Foreign Affairs,
Washington, DC.

The subcommittee met, pursuant to notice, at 2 o'clock p.m., in room 2172 Rayburn House Office Building, Hon. Christopher Smith (chairman of the subcommittee) presiding.

Mr. SMITH. The subcommittee will come to order, and good afternoon to everyone.

As we all know, Boko Haram has significantly accelerated its acts of mass murder and abduction in Nigeria, requiring a more robust and effective response from the Government of Nigeria and friends like the United States.

According to the most recent report by the Internal Displacement Monitoring Centre and the Norwegian Refugee Council, there are now some 3.1 million Nigerian internally displaced persons, or IDPs, more than every other country in the world except for Syria and Colombia.

The U.N. High Commissioner for Refugees estimates that there are now more than 10,000 Nigerian refugees in Niger and Cameroon. According to the International Rescue Committee, due to credible fears of abduction, as many as 1,000 refugees a week, 80 percent women and girls, are fleeing to the nearby country of Niger from Nigeria's Borno State alone.

Former U.S. Ambassador to Nigeria Robin Renee Sanders testified before this subcommittee on June 11 that the fight against Boko Haram will be a "long war," as she put it, but that the Nigerian military and security forces are insufficiently trained and ill-equipped to meet the challenge of a savage, relentless violence unleashed by Boko Haram.

Just this morning she told a Capitol Hill forum on Boko Haram that in the vacuum created by delays in training Nigerian forces vigilante groups have now been formed. They have been there, but now they are growing in number, and are themselves committing human rights abuses.

According to the current State Department human rights report, Boko Haram is responsible for the most heinous human rights violations in Nigeria, but that same report tells us that elements of the Nigerian Armed Forces and security apparatus have committed

(1)

serious human rights abuses as well with little or no account-ability.

Even in the face of serious threats to Nigerian and regional security, the U.S. Government, which has a longstanding alliance with the Federal Republic of Nigeria, has experienced some obstacles in providing the security assistance necessary to help our ally address this dire emergency.

Laws our Congress created to prevent our alliance with rogue military and security forces are being blamed, by some, for making our assistance more difficult to provide. But is the law the problem, or, rather, is it how the law is being applied? Or is it that the U.S. has not attempted to train sufficient numbers of human rights vetted Nigerian forces? Or is it the Nigerians themselves not wanting that kind of training?

What is the targeted number for trained Nigerians? For this year and the future, how many trainers have been committed to this task? I believe the Leahy laws are a necessary component of a prudent human rights policy, and today's hearing is in large part intended to find out whether there are legitimate obstacles to their implementation.

At the outset, I would like to make clear that I have long supported human rights vetting to allow for training of those who pass muster. One example of many, as chair of the then-Subcommittee on International Operations and Human Rights, I chaired a hearing on Indonesia on May 7, 1998, featuring a man by the name of Pius Lustrilanang, who was tortured by members of the Indonesian military amid deep concerns that those involved may have been trained under our Military Education and Training Program, or IMET.

In like manner, I and others were concerned that U.S.-trained Indonesian troops may have been complicit in slaughtering people in East Timor. On a fact-finding trip to Jakarta, I sought but never received the names of specific individuals trained by the U.S., including members of the elite Kopassus unit, who slaughtered dissidents as the Suharto government fell.

Similar training concerns were expressed by me and others concerning the Joint Combined Exchange Training, or JCET, and the Rwandan Patriotic Army during the period when the RPA was engaged in the killing of refugees in Zaire, now the Democratic Republic of the Congo.

Moreover, in 1999, Congress passed my legislation—and Ms. Massimino will remember this well, because she testified at several of those hearings that we had—that suspended all U.S. Federal law enforcement support and exchanges with the British police force in Northern Island, known as the Royal Ulster Constabulary, until the new human rights training programs were implemented there, and until programs were established to vet out any RUC officers who engaged in human rights abuses from benefiting from American training and preparation.

The vetting legislation worked. Exchanges and training at FBI facilities for RUC officers were suspended for more than 2 years, until President Bush certified that the British had established a system to vet and block anyone who committed or condoned human rights violations from the program.

As my colleagues know, according to the current Quadrennial Defense Review, we are in a time of increased danger from terrorist forces in foreign nations, while shrinking budgets force our military and security forces to become smaller and leaner.

The QDR states, and I quote in pertinent part, ''The Department of Defense will rebalance our counterterrorism efforts toward greater emphasis on building partnership capacity, especially in fragile states.'' One manifestation of that developing policy is the President's proposal to allocate $5 billion to a new counterterrorism partnership fund.

I have visited Nigeria twice in the past 9 months alone and have chaired several hearings on security in Nigeria in the past two Congresses alone. Just last month I met with U.S. and Nigerian officials to find out why our security assistance has been so difficult to provide when the need is so increasingly great. Is it the process, or has the administration not sought to seriously expand training? I don't know.

You will notice that the Department of State is not testifying today. That is partly because Assistant Secretary of State for Democracy, Human Rights, and Labor, Tom Malinowski, was unavailable when we invited him to testify. And I know he will come at a future date and hopefully very soon. But it may also be partly due to an abundance of caution surrounding even a discussion of difficulties experienced in implementing the Leahy laws.

For example, when I was in Abuja last month, I asked our Embassy to provide me with their best recommendations, and I would share it with everyone here, for making the Leahy vetting more effective, so that we can provide the much needed aid to the Nigerian Government and end the increasing slaughter and kidnapping of innocents, such as the Chibok schoolgirls. Despite initial assurances of cooperation, I have yet to receive the information, but I will keep asking.

I understand that not everything can be said publicly or should be said publicly, but, again, this law was created with full transparency, passed the Senate at the behest of Senator Leahy, and has been renewed year in and year out, often with tweaks and changes to it.

As my colleagues know, we refer to the Leahy laws because there are actually two of them, one for the Department of State and one for the Department of Defense. Together they cover material assistance, including equipment and training. These laws require investigation of alleged human rights violations by military and security forces, including police.

These investigations performed mostly by the Department of State require details on not only individuals but also military units. Failure to obtain such information as name and date and place of birth can sometimes prevent an investigation and put it into limbo.

National government officials may consider such information an invasion of their sovereignty, although we ought to do more to convince them why that is not so, but to avoid aiding and abetting rogue elements, we must know if a perpetrator of abuse is a man from Jos or a man with the same name from Kano State, as one example.

If individuals or elements of a larger force are guilty of human rights violations, entire battalions or regimens can be tainted unless the guilty are identified and separated out from those forces that are innocent of such crimes. The Leahy laws allow for the recreation of clean units. On the surface, it would seem that such a policy is clear and possible to implement. Unfortunately, it has not been so simple in practice.

Despite the fact that Sarah Sewall, Under Secretary of State for Civilian Security, Democracy, and Human Rights told the full Foreign Affairs Committee on May 21 in this room that at least half of the Nigerian military and security forces are clear of allegations of human rights violations, we continue to be told that Leahy vetting is at least slowing the provision of security assistance.

According to Congressional testimony by Principal Deputy Assistant Secretary of State Robert Jackson, there are an estimated 187 Nigerian military units and 173 police units that have been cleared, but very few Nigerian units have been trained or are in training today. Again, the big question: Why?

Our Government provides approximately $15 billion in security assistance worldwide each year, involving 158 countries, yet there are only 13 headquarters staff handling Leahy vetting, in addition to Embassy personnel. Is this a sign that these laws are not being taken seriously enough by our own Government and is there a requirement for additional spending?

In the current fiscal year, the Department of State is receiving $2.75 million to conduct Leahy vetting. In the newest bill, the Senate has $5 million. Perhaps that will be enough; I don't know. I would hope our distinguished witnesses will shed some light on that.

Of the 158 countries we provided assistance to, 46 had some aid withheld in 2011. The typical percentage of global Leahy vettings that don't meet requirements is about 1 to 2 percent, with just under 10 percent ''suspended.'' In Fiscal Year 2012, according to testimony from the Congressional Research Service expert, Lauren Ploch, the State Department vetted 1,377 members of the Nigerian security forces. And of that figure, 85 percent were cleared to receive assistance, with 15 percent rejected or suspended.

In Colombia, the government rejected the requirements of the Leahy laws before changing their minds and accepting the process. Now there reportedly are more high-ranking Colombian and military officials and officers behind bars than in any other country other than Argentina, and Colombia is cited as a Leahy law success.

In Nigeria, there have been no disciplinary actions against Nigerian military for scorched earth assaults on populations, and few high-ranking Nigerian military officers have been held accountable for human rights violations.

We are here today to examine the questions that these facts raise, and other facts, and our witnesses have been asked to walk us through the process, tell us what works and what doesn't, and suggest ways to make this process more effective.

I would like to now turn to my distinguished colleague, Mr. Cicilline, for any opening he might have.

Mr. CICILLINE. Thank you, Mr. Chairman. And thank you to you and Ranking Member Bass for calling this important and timely hearing.

As we all know, the security situation in Nigeria has deteriorated seriously in recent months with the expansion of Boko Haram, which in April brazenly kidnapped hundreds of young schoolgirls. This committee and this Congress passed a resolution condemning these kidnappings, and I think we all remain committed to providing as much U.S. assistance and advice as can be effective to support the Nigerian Government's efforts to secure the return of these schoolgirls and to stem the violence of this brutal and violent terrorist organization.

Maintaining robust enforcement of the Leahy laws, which serves as the primary safeguard, assuring that the United States is not contributing to human rights violations through its military foreign assistance is, I believe, a necessity if we are to maintain credibility with local populations, not to mention do the right thing by ensuring that we are not supporting or assisting those violating basic human rights.

So I look forward to hearing the testimony today, and I am particularly interested in hearing our witnesses address how we can move forward in a constructive way to assist the Nigerian Government while ensuring that the units we support honor the most basic tenets of human rights and international law.

With that, I thank you, Mr. Chairman, and yield.

Mr. SMITH. Thank you. I would like to yield to Mr. Pittenger.

Mr. PITTENGER. Thank you, Mr. Chairman. Thank you for allowing me to participate in this important hearing and for your 30 years of dedicated commitment to the plight of human rights and religious liberties and freedoms of conscience throughout the world.

Thank you, witnesses, for appearing before us today.

The purpose of this hearing, clearly, is very important, as we work to ensure that we are taking appropriate actions to curb human rights violations around the world, while at the same time not undermining our own national security, the continued attacks aimed at the young girls, then kidnapping and selling those girls into human trafficking, is the most egregious act and cannot be tolerated.

In May, I sent a letter to the President, joined by over 170 of my colleagues, urging all possible action to find and protect those girls. The issue we face, however, is what actions can or should we be taking to support a foreign military who has been continually engaged in politically motivated killings, torture, and excessive use of force, or that have just been negligent in securing their country from those who engage in this egregious abuse.

I look forward to your testimony as we will be considering the issue on the House floor in the coming weeks.

Thank you, Mr. Chairman, and I yield back.

Mr. SMITH. Thank you. I would like to yield to our ranking member, Karen Bass from California.

Ms. BASS. Thank you, Mr. Chair, for holding this hearing. I look forward to the testimony of our witnesses today, and I don't want to take a lot of time. I want to jump right into it. But I am hoping that as part of the testimony and looking at the subject of human rights that someone will address the issue and legislation that is occurring in regards to LGBT individuals and the way we have seen draconian legislation passed in a variety of places, and hopefully you will comment to that in your testimony.

Mr. SMITH. I would like to now introduce our distinguished witnesses, beginning with Ms. Lauren Blanchard, who is a specialist in African affairs at the Congressional Research Service, where she provides analysis on African political, military, and diplomatic affairs, and on U.S. policy in the region, to Members of Congress, committees, and staff.

She has written extensively on security issues and U.S. military engagement on the continent, speaks regularly at academic institutions and international policy fora in the United States and abroad, and has conducted training in various countries across Africa for parliamentarians and other government officials on the policy-making role of the Congress. Previously, she worked at USAID, as well as in the United States Senate.

We will then hear from Colonel Peter Aubrey, who is currently the president of Strategic Opportunities International and has served in a variety of staff and command assignments during both peacetime and war. He served as the initial director of security cooperation for the U.S. Army in Africa, previously served as an Army attache in Nigeria and many other countries across Africa, including Burundi at the height of its civil war.

During the Gulf War, Colonel Aubrey advised Saudi troops and commanded special forces in combat, and he has been awarded the Bronze Star for Valor. Thank you for your distinguished service.

We will then hear from Mr. Stephen Rickard, who directs the Open Society's Washington office advocates working on both U.S. domestic and international issues. He has had a distinguished Washington career on Capitol Hill in the State Department and with human rights organizations.

Before joining Open Society, he created and managed the Freedom Investment Project, working to encourage U.S. support for international justice. Mr. Rickard served as director of the Robert F. Kennedy Memorial Center for Human Rights and as Washington director for Amnesty International USA. And he, too, is no stranger to this committee, and when he was in that position in particular often came up on the Hill and advised us and testified. Prior to that, he worked at the U.S. Department of State, as well as in the U.S. Senate.

We will then hear from Ms. Elisa Massimino, who has been the president and chief executive officer of Human Rights First since 2008, and she helped established the Washington office in 1991 and served as the organization's Washington director from 1997 through 2008. She has a distinguished record of human rights advocacy in Washington, as a national authority in human rights law and policy.

She has testified before Congress dozens of times, and I think at least a dozen before my subcommittee, including this subcommittee, and writes frequently for mainstream publications and specialized journals. The Washington newspaper, the Hill, has repeatedly named her as one of the most effective public advocates in the country.

And, finally, we will hear from Sarah Margon, who is the Washington director of Human Rights Watch. Prior to joining Human Rights Watch, she was associate director of Sustainable Security and Peace Building at the Center for American Progress, where she researched and wrote on a wide range of issues, including human rights, foreign aid, good governance, and global conflicts and crises.

She also served in the U.S. Senate as staff director of the Senate Subcommittee on Africa Affairs, became a senior policy advisor for Oxfam America, and worked at the Open Society Institute.

Ms. Blanchard, if you would begin.

STATEMENT OF MS. LAUREN PLOCH BLANCHARD, SPECIALIST IN AFRICAN AFFAIRS, CONGRESSIONAL RESEARCH SERVICE

Ms. BLANCHARD. Chairman Smith, Ranking Member Bass, and distinguished members of the subcommittee, thank you for inviting CRS to testify today. In my brief statement this afternoon, I will focus on the laws that require human rights vetting and their application in Nigeria. I would ask that my written testimony be submitted for the record.

Mr. SMITH. Without objection, so ordered.

Ms. BLANCHARD. The State Department vets foreign security force units prior to providing U.S. assistance based on policy concerns and to comply with two legal provisions named for their original sponsor, Senator Patrick Leahy. They are just two of the many laws that Congress has enacted to promote human rights and to protect the U.S. image abroad by distancing the United States from abusive governments and security forces.

The first provision is codified in the Foreign Assistance Act and applies to foreign aid programs and those authorized under the Arms Export Control Act. It prohibits assistance to foreign security force units credibly implicated in gross human rights abuses.

The second provision, which applies to security assistance funded through DoD, has appeared in annual defense appropriations acts since 1998. Both provisions have been modified over time, as have the procedures for human rights vetting.

The State Department and DoD Leahy provisions are similar, but not identical, and in recent years legislation has brought the two provisions closer together. The foreign aid provisions apply to all forms of assistance. The DoD provision initially applied only to training, but was expanded in the past year to include equipment and other assistance.

Some differences remain, notably in the standards for the remediation of units deemed ineligible for assistance, and in the exceptions and existence of a waiver authority in the DoD provision. The FAA provision allows no exception from the law except through the credible remediation of the tainted unit, although aid could be provided through measures framed in law with notwithstanding provisions.

The DoD Leahy provision, on the other hand, includes exceptions for equipment and other assistance ''necessary to assist in disaster relief operations or other humanitarian international emergencies.'' The DoD provision also allows the Secretary of Defense to waive the provision in extraordinary circumstances. To date, however, DoD has never issued a waiver, suggesting a very high bar for use.

Despite the differences in the two laws, in practice DoD and the State Department general implement the Leahy laws similarly. Leahy vetting is a multi-stage process that begins at U.S. Embassies abroad and concludes at State Department headquarters. During the process, the names of potential candidates for U.S. assistance are checked against a variety of sources for derogatory information. In the past 2 years, the process has resulted in an approval rate for more than 90 percent of candidates and in an outright denial for fewer than 1 percent.

Growing DoD emphasis on partnering with foreign militaries to address threats such as terrorism has brought increased attention to the Leahy laws. Some military commanders have implied in some cases that the laws have complicated their ability to build foreign counterterrorism and counternarcotics capabilities. Others suggest that U.S. training could improve the behavior of abuse of forces by imparting U.S. values and respect for human rights and the rule of law.

Attention to Leahy laws may intensify as DoD and the State Department determine what effect the new broader DoD Leahy provision will have on security assistance overseas. The expanded provision is repeated in the House version of the FY15 Defense Appropriations Act, and the Senate Armed Services Committee has proposed to codify the provision this year.

As recent hearings have highlighted, the United States is currently seeking to balance security and human rights concerns in Nigeria. U.S. security assistance to Nigeria has been constrained by both law and policy concerns, and the security relationship has been hampered at times by a lack of cooperation from Nigerian officials and by systemic problems in the Nigerian military.

Nigerian security force abuses in the context of operations to counter Boko Haram have complicated efforts to pursue greater cooperation despite shared concerns about the group. Political and human rights concerns have been a prominent factor in shaping U.S.-Nigeria relations for decades.

State Department reports have continued to highlight serious human rights violations by the Nigerian security forces for every year since the transition from military rule in 1999. According to the State Department, the information on security force abuses currently implicates roughly half the units in the Nigerian military, and likely would render those units ineligible for assistance if they were submitted for vetting.

Despite restrictions on some units, U.S. security assistance to Nigeria is sizeable by regional standards, totaling almost $20 million in FY2012 State Department funding, and $16 million in FY2013. DoD funding for Nigeria has been limited, but appears set to expand under a proposed New Global Security Contingency Fund Program.

Multiple systemic factors constrain the effectiveness of the Nigerian security force response to Boko Haram; notably, security sector corruption and mismanagement. Some of these factors impede U.S. support, even for units cleared for assistance. Many soldiers, particularly those in the northeast, reportedly suffer from low morale, and they have struggled to keep pace with a foe that is increasingly well armed and well trained.

By many accounts, Nigerian troops are not adequately resourced or equipped to counter the insurgency, despite a security budget approaching $6 billion. In the assessment of DoD officials, Nigerian funding for the military is skimmed off the top.

DoD officials have assessed the Nigerian forces as ''slow to adapt to new strategies, new doctrines, and new tactics,'' and have described Nigeria as ''an extremely challenging partner to work with.'' U.S. officials have sought to encourage the government to take a more comprehensive counterterrorism approach, and one that is, in the words of one of DoD official to Congress, less brutal. One of the primary aims of DoD engagement is to ''convince the Nigerians to change their tactics, techniques, and procedures in the northeast.''

The State Department suggests that the Leahy laws have provided a strategic tool to encourage reforms in Nigeria, and in Africa more broadly. The Nigerian military has sought to develop its own civilian protection and human rights monitoring and training in the past year, and the Nigerian President recently ordered more human rights training for officers.

Nigerian officials have also made statements suggesting an evolving counterterrorism strategy, one that seeks not only security but also political and economic solutions. In sum, Nigeria provides an example of the challenges U.S. policymakers face in building foreign counterterrorism capacities.

By many accounts, developing countries like Nigeria that are struggling with terrorist threats may desperately need the specialized skills and support that U.S. security assistance is designed to provide. But when security forces abuse civilians, U.S. engagement may risk not only tainting the U.S. image, but also may fuel popular grievances and alienate local populations.

U.S. officials continue to explore ways to improve the vetting process in the dialogue with partner governments to enhance effectiveness in accountability and to mitigate the risk that U.S. partners might not use U.S. assistance responsibly.

Thank you, and I look forward to your questions.

[The prepared statement of Ms. Blanchard follows:]

Statement of Lauren Ploch Blanchard
Specialist in African Affairs
Congressional Research Service

Before

The House Foreign Affairs Subcommittee on Africa, Global Health, Global Human Rights, and International Organizations

Hearing: "Human Rights Vetting: Nigeria and Beyond"
July 10, 2014

Chairman Smith, Ranking Member Bass, and distinguished Members of the subcommittee, thank you for inviting the Congressional Research Service to testify today. As requested, I will focus my remarks today on the so-called "Leahy laws," which prohibit the provision of U.S. security assistance to foreign security force units that have been credibly implicated in gross violations of human rights, and on the laws' application in the context of U.S.-Nigeria security cooperation.[1]

Forty years ago, Congress expressed the position in legislation that the United States should condition security assistance to foreign countries based on their human rights records, and in 1976, Congress passed legislation declaring that promoting increased observance of human rights was a principal goal of U.S. foreign policy.[2] Decades later, Congress continues to deliberate on how best to achieve this aim amidst other foreign policy and national security objectives, including notably, countering the threats of terrorism and violent extremism, weapons proliferation, and regional instability.

The Leahy Laws

The State Department evaluates, or "vets," foreign security force units prior to providing U.S. assistance based on policy concerns and to comply with two legal provisions known collectively as the Leahy laws for their original sponsor, Senator Patrick Leahy. The first

---

[1] This statement draws from various CRS products, including CRS Reports R43361, *"Leahy Law" Human Rights Provisions and Security Assistance: Issue Overview*, by Nina Serafino, June Beittel, Lauren Ploch Blanchard, and Liana Rosen; and RL33964, *Nigeria: Current Issues and U.S. Policy*; and R43558, *Boko Haram: Frequently Asked Questions*, both by Lauren Ploch Blanchard.

[2] Section 502B(a)(1) of the Foreign Assistance Act of 1961 (P.L.87-195), as amended in 1974 by P.L.93-559, and amended by Section 301(a) of the International Security Assistance and Arms Export Control Act (P.L.94-329) in 1976.

legal provision, which applies to programs funded through State Department and Foreign Operations appropriations, dates back to 1997 and was codified in 2007 in Section 620M of the Foreign Assistance Act of 1961, as amended (hereafter FAA; 22 U.S.C. 2378d).[3] The second legal provision, which applies to security assistance funded through Department of Defense (DOD) appropriations, has appeared in annual defense appropriations acts since 1998. Both provisions have been modified over time, as have the State Department's procedures for human rights vetting.

Legislative Background

The Leahy provisions are just two of the many laws that Congress has enacted to promote respect for human rights and to protect the U.S. image abroad by distancing the United States from corrupt or brutal foreign governments and security forces. A major precursor to the Leahy laws was a 1974 legislative provision, codified as Section 502B of the FAA, which expressed the sense of Congress that the President should "substantially reduce or terminate" security assistance to any government found to have a "consistent pattern" of gross human rights violations.[4] Section 502B was amended in 1976 and strengthened to prohibit such assistance unless "extraordinary circumstances" warrant its provision.[5] Various other country-specific legal provisions related to security assistance and human rights concerns predate the Leahy laws. Congress has continued to enact new restrictions on security assistance to certain countries through provisions in annual appropriations and country-specific or issue-specific authorizations.

The human rights vetting process required under Section 620M of the FAA has its origins in a section of the FY1997 foreign aid appropriations measure (P.L.104-208) that restricted the obligation of State Department counter-narcotics funds to foreign security force units for which the Secretary of State had "credible evidence" of serious abuses. That provision was expanded the following year to cover all forms of security assistance appropriated in the FY1998 foreign operations bill (P.L. 105-118).[6] Thereafter, the provision appeared in annual foreign operations appropriations until it was codified in 2007 (P.L. 110-161, 22 U.S.C. 2378d).

In 1998, Congress placed a similar condition in the FY1999 defense appropriations bill, to prohibit the use of DOD funds to train foreign security force units implicated in gross

---

[3] The FAA serves as the overarching legal authorization for U.S. foreign assistance policies and programs. The FAA Leahy provision applies to assistance authorized by the FAA and the Arms Export Control Act, as amended (AECA, P.L. 90-629).

[4] Section 502B was originally added to the FAA in the Foreign Assistance Act of 1974 (P.L.93-559) and amended in 1976 under P.L. 94-329. Another early congressional effort to legislate on human rights and military assistance was Section 32 of the Foreign Assistance Act of 1973.

[5] State Department officials indicate that the Section 502B prohibition has rarely, if ever, been invoked, because it is viewed as ambiguous.

[6] Congress passed the FY1998 provision in spite of concerns expressed by some Members of the House of Representatives over its possible impact on Colombia's drug interdiction efforts. An early test of the expanded provision was a State Department decision in December 1998 to reject a request for a U.S. loan guarantee by the U.S. Export-Import Bank for armored vehicles for certain units of the Turkish police force, based on human rights concerns. It is not clear whether the Clinton Administration at the time determined that such a loan would be a violation of the law, or whether the rejection was undertaken for policy reasons and/or in anticipation of congressional opposition. See Dana Priest, "New Human Rights Law Triggers Policy Debate," *Washington Post*, December 31, 1998.

human rights violations. Unlike the foreign aid provision, which applied to all forms of assistance (unless exempted by legal authority permitting such assistance "notwithstanding" any other provision of law, as exists for several international security assistance accounts), the DOD provision initially applied specifically to training, but was expanded in the FY2014 defense appropriations bill (P.L. 113-76) to also include equipment and "other assistance" to foreign security force units.

The State Department and DOD Leahy provisions are similar, but not identical, and in recent years, legislation has brought the language in the two provisions closer together.[7] Some differences remain: in the standards for the remediation of units "tainted" (determined ineligible for assistance) by allegations of gross human rights violations; in the FAA provision's requirement of a "duty to inform" foreign governments of the basis for withholding assistance; and in the exceptions and existence of a waiver authority in the DOD provision.[8] The FAA Leahy provision allows no exception from the prohibition of assistance except through the credible remediation of the tainted unit (though aid could be made available through foreign operations appropriations and authorization measures framed as "notwithstanding" provisions), while the DOD provision includes exceptions for equipment or other assistance "necessary to assist in disaster relief operations or other humanitarian or national emergencies." The DOD provision also allows the Secretary of Defense to waive the prohibition in "extraordinary circumstances." While that term is not defined in law, DOD officials indicate that a waiver has never been issued, based on an understanding with congressional Appropriators that the bar for waiving the vetting requirement would be very high.[9] Despite these differences in the two laws, in practice, DOD and the State Department generally implement the Leahy laws similarly.

Implementation: The Vetting Process[10]

Congress has vested the State Department's Bureau for Democracy, Human Rights, and Labor (DRL) with responsibility for creating and promoting U.S. government human rights policies. DRL prepares the State Department's annual country reports on human

---

[7] Congress amended the FAA Leahy provision in 2011 (P.L. 112-74), aligning it more closely with the DOD provision by changing the threshold for the prohibition from plural "gross violations" to a singular "gross violation" of human rights, changing the standard of proof from "credible evidence" to "credible information," and modifying the standard to resume aid by requiring the foreign government to take "effective steps" rather than "effective measures" to bring responsible individuals to justice.

[8] The DOD remediation standard requires that "all necessary corrective steps have been taken," while the FAA provision requires that the relevant government be "taking effective steps to bring the responsible members of the security forces unit to justice." Neither remediation standard is defined further in law, although the conference report with P.L. 105-118 explains that the intent of the FAA language is that there be "a credible investigation and that the individuals involved face appropriate disciplinary action or impartial prosecution in accordance with local law." The State Department recently issued new internal policy guidance on the criteria for remediation. The FAA "duty to inform" provision requires the Secretary of State to inform a government of the basis for withholding assistance and to help that government, to the extent practicable, take effective measures to bring the responsible individuals to justice.

[9] Communications between CRS and both Appropriators and DOD, November and December 2013.

[10] For more information on the implementation of the Leahy laws, see CRS Report R43361, "Leahy Law" Human Rights Provisions and Security Assistance: Issue Overview and Government Accountability Office (GAO), Human Rights: Additional Guidance, Monitoring, and Training Could Improve Implementation of the Leahy Laws, GAO-13-866, September 2013.

rights practices (as required under Section 502B of the FAA), and it is the lead bureau for managing human rights vetting (a.k.a. "Leahy vetting").

Leahy vetting is a multi-stage process that begins in U.S. embassies abroad and concludes at State Department headquarters. During the process, the names of potential candidates for U.S. assistance are checked against a variety of sources for "derogatory information."[11] The credibility of this information is evaluated on a case-by-case basis and need not meet the standard of evidence required in a U.S. court of law. Both Leahy laws state that assistance should be denied to *units* credibly alleged to have committed gross abuses, and Appropriators have clarified that, even in cases where training is provided on an individual basis, the individual's unit must be vetted as well. In 2010, the State Department began using a dedicated online database system known as INVEST (International Vetting and Security Tracking), facilitating a major increase in the number of individuals and units vetted. Of the more than 330,000 individuals/units vetted globally in the past two years, State Department officials report that the process has resulted in approval for more than 90%, ending in denial for fewer than 1%, and a suspension for less than 9%.[12]

Policy Tensions

Growing DOD emphasis on the potential strategic value of partnering with foreign militaries to address transnational threats such as terrorism has brought increased attention to the application of the Leahy laws from U.S. military officials and from some Members of Congress. Some military commanders have implied that in some cases the laws have complicated their ability to build the counterterrorism and counternarcotics capacities of foreign partners. In March 2013, the commander of U.S. Special Operations Command (SOCOM), Admiral William McRaven, stated in congressional testimony that while he supported the vetting process, it had "restricted us in a number of countries...in our ability to train units that we think need to be trained."[13] In subsequent testimony he indicated that there were efforts underway to improve the process, particularly on assessing the efforts of a foreign government to bring abusive forces to justice so that "tainted" units might be deemed eligible for assistance.[14] Others have argued that U.S. training could improve the behavior of abusive forces by imparting U.S. values and respect for human rights and the rule of law.[15] Many in the human rights community counter that the expansion of DOD "partner capacity building" programs around the

---

[11] Information on the process is available at http://www.humanrights.gov/2013/07/09/an-overview-of-the-leahy-vetting-process/. Section 502B of the FAA mandates that consideration be given to the relevant findings of appropriate international groups, including non-governmental organizations.

[12] A suspension occurs when the host nation or US embassy fails to provide sufficient identifying information or when there are serious questions about a unit that are deemed to require further investigation/consideration.

[13] House Armed Services Committee, hearing to receive testimony on U.S. Central Command and U.S. Special Operations Command in Review of the FY2014 Defense Authorization Request, March 5, 2013.

[14] House Armed Services Subcommittee on Intelligence, Emerging Threats and Capabilities, hearing on FY2014 Defense Authorization Request as it relates to U.S Special Operations Command and U.S. Special Operations Forces, April 17, 2014.

[15] Eric Schmitt, "Military Says Law Barring U.S. Aid to Rights Violators Hurts Training Mission," *New York Times*, June 21, 2013.

world warrants greater scrutiny than ever to ensure that U.S. assistance does not support foreign units implicated in serious abuses.

Attention to the Leahy laws may intensify as DOD and the State Department determine what effect the new, broader DOD Leahy provision contained in P.L. 113-76, which now applies to all DOD "assistance," will have on U.S. security cooperation with partner nations. The provision also may have implications for the implementation of the vetting process itself, as it is likely to add a considerable workload to the existing system. The added workload may raise concerns from those who manage the day-to-day relations with foreign governments, i.e., those who manage security cooperation at U.S. embassies, about longer administrative delays in approving candidates for planned activities.

As outlined in the 2014 Quadrennial Defense Review (QDR), DOD is rebalancing its counterterrorism efforts toward a greater emphasis on building the capacity of foreign partners, and the proposed $5 billion Counterterrorism Partnerships Fund (CTPF) in the Administration's FY2015 Overseas Contingency Operations (OCO) request might significantly expand DOD security assistance-type activities, with possible implications for human rights vetting.[16] The Administration's proposed statutory language for the CTPF would allow DOD to obligate funding "notwithstanding any limitation in a provision of law that would otherwise restrict the amount or recipients of such support or assistance," contingent on notification to Congress that it is in the national security interest to do so.[17]

Despite concerns such as those raised by Admiral McRaven, Congress expanded the scope of the DOD Leahy provision to include not just training, but all DOD assistance in P.L. 113-76. The same language is repeated in the House version of the FY2015 DOD Appropriations Act, H.R. 4870. The Senate Armed Services Committee has proposed to codify the broadened provision in its version of the FY2015 National Defense Authorization Act, S. 2410.[18] The bill would define "other assistance" as that which has as its "primary purpose" building the capacity of a foreign security force.

While there do not appear to have been any major recent legislative efforts to roll back the Leahy provisions, questions posed by this committee and others indicate that U.S. government perspectives on the laws vary.[19] National Security Advisor Susan Rice alluded to debates within the executive branch surrounding human rights laws in remarks to human rights advocates in late 2013, stating,

---

[16] The 2014 QDR states, "The ability to project forces to combat terrorism in places as far away as Yemen, Afghanistan, and Mali – and to build capacity to help partners counter terrorism and counter the proliferation of weapons of mass destruction (WMD) – reduces the likelihood that these threats could find their way to U.S. shores." For concerns about the CTPF and human rights vetting, see, e.g., "U.S. Should Aid Those Who Fight Terror, Not Abet Human Rights Abuses," *Washington Post*, July 7, 2014.

[17] White House, FY2015 Budget Amendments for the Department of Defense and the Department of State and Other International Programs to Fund Overseas Contingency Operations, June 26, 2014.

[18] The relevant language in S. 2410 is the same as that in P.L. 113-76, but with an added exception in the event that the assistance is necessary "to conduct human rights training of foreign security forces."

[19] See, e.g., questions raised in House Armed Services Committee, *The Proposed FY2014 Defense Authorization as it Relates to U.S. Central Command and U.S. Special Operations*, March 6, 2013. See also, Emily Cadei, "Foreign Militaries, Domestic Tension," *CQ Weekly*, December 16, 2013.

15

We sometimes face painful dilemmas when the immediate need to defend our national security clashes with our fundamental commitment to democracy and human rights. Let's be honest: at times, as a result, we do business with governments that do not respect the rights we hold most dear....I will not pretend that some short-term tradeoffs do not exist....the fact is: American foreign policy must sometimes strike a difficult balance—not between our values and interests, because these almost invariably converge with time, but more often between our short and long-term imperatives.[20]

As recent congressional hearings have highlighted, the U.S. government currently is seeking to find that "difficult balance" in Nigeria, where security forces abuses in the context of operations to counter one of the world's deadliest terrorist groups, Boko Haram, have complicated U.S. efforts to pursue greater counterterrorism cooperation, despite shared concerns about Boko Haram and its ties to transnational terrorist groups.

The Nigerian Context

U.S. security assistance to Nigeria has been constrained both by law and by policy concerns, and the security relationship also has been hampered at times by a lack of cooperation from Nigerian officials and by systemic problems in the Nigerian military. Political and human rights concerns have been a prominent factor in shaping U.S.-Nigeria relations for decades. The country was ruled by the military for much of the four decades after independence, and U.S. sanctions—some imposed under an executive order and others consistent with appropriations legislation—prohibited security assistance to Nigeria for most of the 1990s.[21]

The bilateral relationship has improved significantly since Nigeria's transition to civilian rule in 1999, although State Department human rights reports have continued to highlight serious human rights violations by the Nigerian security forces in every year since the transition. These violations include politically motivated and extrajudicial killings, excessive use of force, and torture. The summary execution of suspects by joint security force operations against both Niger Delta militants in the south and Boko Haram in the northeast has been a common theme in State Department reporting. There is little, if any, evidence to indicate that the government has held those responsible for abuses accountable for their actions.[22]

Nigerian security force abuses, particularly those committed in the northeast in the context of operations to counter Boko Haram, have been documented by journalists, human rights advocates, and others, including foreign governments like the United States, among others.[23] This derogatory information, according to the State Department,

---

[20] Remarks by National Security Advisor Susan E. Rice, "Human Rights: Advancing American Interests and Values," Human Rights First Annual Summit, Washington DC, December 4, 2013.
[21] Among other sanctions, the Clinton Administration suspended arms sales and military aid to Nigeria after the military government annulled the 1993 election. Recurring language in annual foreign operations appropriations (currently Sec. 7008 of P.L.113-76) prohibits the provision of economic or security assistance to governments that have come to power through a coup. There is no waiver for that prohibition.
[22] The State Department's most recent human rights report, covering 2013, stated the inability to verify any disciplinary charges for human rights abuses in the context of security force operations in the northeast.
[23] In detailing security force abuses in the northeast, the State Department's most recent human rights report states that "while press articles often contained contradictory and inaccurate information, multiple

implicates roughly half the units in the Nigerian army, and likely would render those units ineligible for security assistance if they were to be submitted for vetting.[24] The United States is not the only donor government that has restricted security assistance based on human rights concerns; the United Kingdom, once a major provider of training and equipment to the Nigerian military, has significantly reduced its assistance in recent years, and the sale of lethal weapons to Nigeria is now prohibited under UK law.[25]

Despite restrictions on assistance to some units, U.S. security assistance to Nigeria is sizable by regional standards, totaling almost $20 million in FY2012 State Department funding and $16 million in FY2013. Nigeria also acquires U.S. defense materiel through U.S. Foreign Military Sales (FMS), Direct Commercial Sales (DCS), and Excess Defense Articles (EDA). DOD funding for Nigeria is limited and largely focused on counternarcotics support; military cooperation appears strongest with the Nigerian navy.

In FY2012, the State Department vetted 1,377 members of the Nigerian security forces—of that figure, almost 85% were cleared to receive assistance, while 15% were rejected or suspended.[26] (Being approved to receive assistance in a given fiscal year does not necessarily denote actual participation in a U.S.-funded program.)

Proponents of human rights vetting argue that the main impediment to U.S. efforts to support Nigeria's broader response to Boko Haram is not the Leahy laws, but gross violations committed by the Nigerian forces, the Nigerian government's resistance to adopting a more comprehensive approach to Boko Haram, and the continued lack of political will within the government to investigate allegations of human rights abuses and hold perpetrators accountable. The Nigerian government also has appeared reticent in some cases to allow its security forces to participate in U.S. training programs. The State Department indicates that there are currently 187 Nigerian military units and 173 police units that have been vetted and cleared to receive U.S. assistance and training.[27] Significantly, given the context of U.S. efforts to assist Nigerian operations to rescue hundreds of schoolgirls kidnapped by Boko Haram, among the cleared units are two that the State Department views as best positioned to conduct hostage rescue operations—the Special Boat Service commando unit and the 101st Infantry Battalion—but both reportedly require significant additional training. It is unclear whether the Nigerian

---

sources confirmed allegations of abuses." Recent reports on abuses include Michelle Faul, "Nigeria's Military Killing Thousands of Detainees, *Associated Press*, October 18, 2013; Human Rights Watch, *Spiraling Violence: Boko Haram Attacks and Security Force Abuses in Nigeria*, October 2012 and "Massive Destruction, Deaths from Military Raid," Press Release, May 1, 2013; Amnesty International, *Nigeria: More than 1,500 Killed in Armed Conflict in North-Eastern Nigeria in Early 2014*, March 31, 2014, *Stop Torture—Country Profile: Nigeria*, May 13, 2014, and *Nigeria: Trapped in the Cycle of Violence*, August 2012; and *Criminal Force: Torture, Abuse, and Extrajudicial Killings by the Nigerian Police Force*, by the Open Society Justice Initiative and the Network of Police Reform in Nigeria.

[24] Testimony of State Department Under Secretary for Civilian Security, Democracy, and Human Rights Sarah Sewell, House Foreign Affairs Committee, *Boko Haram: The Growing Threat to Schoolgirls, Nigeria, and Beyond*, May 21, 2014.

[25] Andrew Walker, "Why Nigeria Has Not Defeated Boko Haram," *BBC*, May 14, 2014.

[26] State Department Office of Inspections, *Inspection of Embassy Abuja and Consulate General Lagos, Nigeria*, ISP-I-13-16A, February 2013.

[27] Answer to Questions for the Record Submitted to Principal Deputy Assistant Secretary Robert Jackson by Senator Chris Coons, Senate Foreign Relations Committee, May 15, 2014.

government has given approval for such training to occur. A 2013 State Department audit report noted that, in addition to human rights concerns, the Nigerians' late submission of names of candidates for assistance was a "recurring problem" for the U.S. embassy.[28]

Multiple systemic factors further constrain the effectiveness of the Nigerian security force response to Boko Haram, notably security sector corruption and mismanagement, and some of these factors impede U.S. support even for units that have been cleared for assistance.[29] Soldiers, particularly in the northeast, reportedly suffer from low morale, struggling to keep pace with a foe that is reportedly increasingly well-armed and trained. By many accounts, Nigerian troops are not adequately resourced or equipped to counter the insurgency, despite a security budget totaling almost $5.8 billion.[30] In the assessment of DOD officials, Nigerian funding for the military is "skimmed off the top."[31]

DOD officials have assessed the Nigerian forces as "slow to adapt with new strategies, new doctrines and new tactics," and have described Nigeria as "an extremely challenging partner to work with."[32] U.S. officials have sought to encourage the Nigerian government to take a more comprehensive approach to countering the Boko Haram threat, and one which is, in the words of one DOD official, "less brutal."[33] When Secretary of State John Kerry visited the region last year, he raised these concerns with Nigerian officials, stating, "one person's atrocity does not excuse another's."[34] "When soldiers destroy towns, kill civilians and detain innocent people with impunity, mistrust takes root," another State Department official recently told the Senate.[35] One of the primary aims of recent DOD engagement is to "convince the Nigerians to change their tactics, techniques, and procedures toward Boko Haram," and toward that end the U.S. military team that has deployed to Nigeria to assist in tracking down the kidnapped schoolgirls will seek to analyze the Nigerian operations and identify gaps for which international experts can provide assistance.[36] To date, despite some positive public comments from U.S. officials about "a growing level of cooperation," it remains unclear to what extent Nigerian officials are cooperating with foreign advisors and experts, including the team that the Administration deployed in May.[37]

---

[28] State Department Office of Inspections, *Inspection of Embassy Abuja and Consulate General Lagos, Nigeria*, ISP-I-13-16A, February 2013.

[29] The State Department's 2013 Country Report on Terrorism notes a lack of coordination and cooperation between Nigerian security agencies; corruption; misallocation of resources; limited requisite databases; the slow pace of the judicial system; and lack of sufficient training for prosecutors and judges to implement anti-terrorism laws.

[30] Tim Cocks, "Boko Haram Exploits Nigeria's Slow Military Decline," *Reuters*, May 9, 2014; and Adam Nossiter, "Nigeria's Army Hampers Hunt for Abducted Schoolgirls," *New York Times*, May 23, 2014.

[31] Testimony of DOD Principal Director for African Affairs Alice Friend, Senate Subcommittee on African Affairs, *#BringBackOurGirls: Addressing the Threat of Boko Haram*, May 15, 2014.

[32] Ibid.

[33] Ibid.

[34] "Kerry Criticizes Nigeria on Human Rights," CNN, May 25, 2013.

[35] Testimony of Principal Deputy Assistant Secretary of State for African Affairs Robert P. Jackson, Senate Foreign Relations Committee, *#BringBackOurGirls: Addressing the Threat of Boko Haram*, May 15, 2014.

[36] Testimony of DOD Principal Director for African Affairs Alice Friend, May 15, 2014, op. cit.

[37] Testimony of State Department Under Secretary Sarah Sewell, House Foreign Affairs Committee, Boko Haram: The Growing Threat to Schoolgirls, Nigeria, and Beyond, May 21, 2014.

The State Department suggests the Leahy laws have provided a "strategic" diplomatic tool to encourage reforms in Nigeria, and in Africa more broadly.[38] The Nigerian army has sought assistance in developing its own civilian protection and human rights monitoring and training, and in February 2014 President Goodluck Jonathan issued an order than officers should receive more human rights training.

There also have been some statements by Nigerian officials that suggest an evolving counterterrorism strategy. In March 2014, Nigeria's National Security Advisor unveiled a new "soft approach" to countering the insurgency.[39] He announced the creation of a new Counter Terrorism Center in his office and outlined new measures to improve coordination among the federal, state, and local governments, as well as new counter-radicalization efforts and prison reforms. In early July, the Finance Minister described the government's new "three-pronged" strategy to deal with the Boko Haram crisis, stating that it seeks not only security, but also political and economic solutions.[40] As part of the purported new strategy, she outlined a range of new programs, including one to create jobs for unemployed youth in the states most affected by Boko Haram, and a broader economic empowerment initiative for the northeast. The degree to which these efforts will lead to greater respect for human rights in practice remains to be seen.

In sum, Nigeria provides an example of the challenges U.S. policymakers face in building foreign counterterrorism capacities. "Some of the countries where we have some very, very, important national security interests evolving right now have some of the worst records," DOD's top civilian advisor on special operations told Congress in 2013, and he flagged Nigeria specifically as an example.[41] By many accounts, developing countries like Nigeria that are struggling with terrorist threats may desperately need the specialized skills and support that U.S. security assistance is designed to provide. However, when security forces abuse civilians, U.S. engagement may risk not only tainting the U.S. image abroad, but also may fuel popular grievances and alienate local populations, thereby undermining international efforts to discredit terrorist groups. The issues surrounding human rights vetting therefore touch on both the tactical and strategic aspects of U.S. foreign policy. Both State and DOD officials, in collaboration with interested Members, continue to explore ways to improve both the vetting process and the diplomatic dialogue with partner states to enhance effectiveness and accountability, and to mitigate the risk that U.S. partners might not use U.S. assistance responsibly.

---

[38] Answer to Questions for the Record Submitted to Principal Deputy Assistant Secretary Robert Jackson by Senator Chris Coons, Senate Foreign Relations Committee, May 15, 2014. In an August 2013 letter to African Studies academics, Secretary of State Kerry stated that the Leahy laws "serve as a strategic tool" and that their implementation has "helped us shape African partners' approach to security cooperation and assistance by highlighting the importance of good security sector governance" and "strengthen our ability to combat terrorism and instability in Africa by directing U.S. security assistance to professional forces respectful of human rights norms."

[39] Ronald Mutum, "Nigeria: FG Announces 'Soft' Counter-Terror Strategy," *Daily Trust*, March 19, 2014.

[40] "Boko Haram—FG Has Changed Tactics Says Okonjo-Iweala," *Independent*, July 4, 2014.

[41] Comments by Assistant Secretary of Defense for Special Operations and Low-Intensity Conflict Michael A. Sheehan, House Armed Services Subcommittee on Intelligence, Emerging Threats and Capabilities, hearing, April 17, 2013, op. cit.

Mr. Smith. Thank you very much for your testimony.

I would like to now ask Colonel Aubrey if he would present his comments to the subcommittee.

STATEMENT OF COLONEL PETER AUBREY, USA, RETIRED, PRESIDENT, STRATEGIC OPPORTUNITIES INTERNATIONAL

Colonel Aubrey. Chairman Smith, Ranking Member Bass, distinguished members of the subcommittee, thank you for inviting me here today.

As requested, I will focus my remarks today on what are commonly called the Leahy laws, which prohibit the provision of U.S. security assistance to foreign security force units that have been credibly implicated in violations of human rights.

I previously submitted written comments to the subcommittee and request that they be entered into your record.

Mr. Smith. Without objection, so ordered. And that of all of our distinguished witnesses will be made a part of the record, your statements and any material you would like attached to it.

Colonel Aubrey. Thank you. Rather than reading what I had previously submitted, I would like to give some observations on security assistance that I have encountered in a 30-plus year career that focused on foreign internal defense, security assistance, and security cooperation as they affect training in Nigeria.

Nigeria is a particularly difficult case. During my tour there from 2006 to 2008, I served with three different Chiefs of Army Staff. Two were American-trained, and I enjoyed good access and a large degree of cooperation. The third was not U.S.-trained, was uncooperative, and routinely refused to facilitate vetting for U.S. training, claiming it was an unreasonable infringement of Nigerian sovereignty.

My team and I got the job done. It wasn't pretty, it wasn't prompt, and it definitely wasn't easy. Vetting can be near impossible. The standards are not beyond reasonable doubt, but credible. A misspelled name can result in unintentional blacklisting, and the system does not lend itself to correction. And, more importantly, you have to have the host nation cooperating. If they do not cooperate, the system fails.

There is no simple answer on how to solve vetting, training, and access in Nigeria. Corruption, poor leadership, regional differences, tribal issues, and religious conflicts plague Nigeria and its armed forces.

Previous sanctions have led to a generation of leadership not enamored with the United States, having been trained, mentored, and cultivated by some of our global competitors. Nigeria does not have a command and control infrastructure that will allow its commanders in the field to have direct controls of his forces, relying on cell phones and in some cases runners to pass messages.

Training is inadequate. Soldiers receive an inadequate amount of ammunition to train with. Officers frequently abuse their authorities, and there is no real professional NCO corps.

The units that we have focused our attention on, usually those earmarked for external U.N.-sponsored peacekeeping missions, perform at a much higher standard, but still suffer from the problems I describe. At the same time, the Nigerians are fiercely proud of their accomplishments. They have West Africa's War College. They offer officer training to their neighbors.

They have successfully deployed to neighboring countries, and they participate in regional exercises and deployments. All of these issues help set the stage for the dilemma that is Nigeria and the difficulties faced in providing training to help combat the surge of Islamic extremism in the northeast and their inability to contain the violence.

Nigeria's problems of vetting can be found almost everywhere. In Liberia, the Liberian Armed Forces, a force recruited, vetted, trained, and still mentored by U.S. personnel, still have training delayed by vetting requirements, and we know that their force has not been accused of human rights violations.

The rest of Africa has similar stories. In my written testimony, I passed a story relayed to me by one of my former subordinates that in Uganda a misfire occurred in an attempt to rehabilitate a blacklisted unit. The end result was the blacklisting of the officer involved in the rehabilitation attempt, rather than the rehabilitation of the blacklisted unit.

I offer these following recommendations to the committee for consideration. Authorize DoD human rights training in a broad category of subjects similar to the expanded IMET program that we executed in the 1990s. Allow engagement that is designed to professionalize those errant forces, teach the law of land for human rights, the military role in civil societies, and other such subjects. Develop an exit strategy for the bad units and individuals that will build for the potential for full engagement. Rehabilitate and professionalize, rather than punish. And, finally, develop some type of vetting process for units like the LAF.

If we don't engage, our global competitors can and usually will.

I want to thank this committee for this opportunity, and I stand ready to answer your questions.

[The prepared statement of Colonel Aubrey follows:]

STRATEGIC OPPORTUNITIES INTERNATIONAL

Prepared Statement of

COL Peter W Aubrey USA (ret)
President, Strategic Opportunities International
Before the

The Houe Foreign Affairs Subcommittee on Africa, Global Health, Global Human Rights and International Organization

Hearing: Human Rights Vetting: Nigeria and Beyond

10 July 2014

Chairman Smith, Ranking Member Bass, and distinguished Members of the subcommittee, thank you for inviting me here to testify today of this important matter concerning foreign policy, national security objectives and the training of foreign military forces. Always important, supporting our friends and allies in professionalizing their forces in what has become an era of persistent conflict has become a key component of our National Defense Strategy. This requirement has caused the Department of Defense to emphasize security assistance and security cooperation as a method to achieve this support. One of the components of these engagement strategies is foreign military training. Since the 1990's, a requirement to providing training is the certification on human rights, better known as the Leahy laws.

Designed to promote the "respect for human rights abroad" as well serving as important foreign policy tools, these legal provisions also help safeguard America's image abroad by ensuring that we do not deliberately or accidently train brutal or corrupt defense and security forces. Despite its noble intent, there is a negative side to these provisions. Cumbersome, time consuming validation and vetting of local national forces ensure that a rapid response to emergency training requirements will not occur. Units that are black listed seem to be forever tarnished for the misdeeds of their predecessors and active cooperation at all levels of a local national defense establishment is required. We cannot engage and professionalize a force if it has committed or has been accused of committing actions we find objectionable. Of course, that means that we will not have the opportunity to insert ourselves in professionalization efforts for the force in question or help eradicate that behavior or action we find objectionable or rapidly help in moments of crisis.

During the course of these hearings, you will have the opportunity to listen to experts who will discuss legal, human rights and foreign policy that can explain in detail the provisions, the requirements and restrictions as well of the benefits of this law. What I can offer is complimentary views, the viewpoint of the guy on the ground that has spent years trying to facilitate and execute U.S. foreign policy and national security goals and objectives from while serving as the U.S. Defense Attaché office, executing security cooperation at the Theater Army level, from the viewpoint of the previous commander of the Army's designated security assistance training command.

STRATEGIC OPPORTUNITIES INTERNATIONAL

Examples

Nigeria: Between 2006 and 2008, I was the senior military representative to the Gulf of Guinea Energy Security Talks. The principal military force earmarked for the protection of the oil fields and pipelines was the Joint Task Force. Set up in 2004 to restore order in the Niger Delta, the JTF was composed Nigerian army, navy, air force and mobile police elements. From almost the beginning, this JTF was accused of excessive force, human rights violations including extrajudicial executions, torture and destruction of homes believed to have harbored militants. By late 2007, the situation had deteriorated further, with foreigners and expatriates routinely kidnapped and the oil installations threatened. Assistance requested included communications equipment, boats and training. At that time, the U.S. was importing approximately 10% of our oil consumption from Nigeria. Because of the allegations of human rights violations as well as Nigerian unwillingness to grant U.S. access to the region in question, we were unable to meet any of the assistance requests to help secure this vital resource and still unresolved by the time I departed. This inability to assist when requested did but strain on our bilateral relationships.

The Leahy Law restrictions on engagement were compounded by previous sanctions and a poor command and control infrastructure. Prior restrictions to engagement has led to a generation of Nigerian leaders who do not know us, having received professional education from some of our competitors. In some cases, I was faced with offering limited assistance not necessarily in line with what was requested, to people who didn't like us to start off. The Nigerian C2 infrastructure frequently failed, did not give real time updates and frequently led to a disconnect between units in the field and their command infrastructure. Ajuba did not control its units in the Delta and the command infrastructure in the Delta had little influence on the activities of its units as they deployed from their home bases. It is important to remember that in many cases, engagement equal access. Units and services I could offer training to, I had access and I could assist in the professionalization of those units.

Uganda. Another example of issues with Leahy vetting was passed to me by my former security assistance chief in Nigeria, LTC Lu Perozo, USA (ret) from his recent service in Uganda as the U.S. Defense Attaché. LTC Perozo stated that he had been approached by the AFRICOM J2 who wanted to expand the level of cooperation with the Chieftaincy of Military Intelligence (CMI). The AFRICOM objective was to improve Ugandan capabilities in two areas: AMISOM and counter LRA. Both were/are USG priorities. As the DAO and AFRICOM looked at ways to do this (train and equip), it was soon realized that Leahy vetting was an issue. Sections within the organization and the incumbent Chief, a serving Brigadier General, would not pass vetting. As a measure of cooperation the Chief was replaced. His successor was a U.S. trained officer with a great reputation who wanted to implement some reforms at CMI. The initial thought was that this change would allow forward movement. Instead the new Chief was also deemed a "bad guy" because now he was part of the unit. This made it all the way up to President Museveni and the Commander of Land Forces. Needless to say it created all sorts of issues for the

STRATEGIC OPPORTUNITIES INTERNATIONAL

United States in implementing just about every program. The Commander Land Forces stated it simply, "If you don't want to help us we'll just ask Russia and China."

Liberia. At the beginning of this century, this small West African country's army was, at best, a mess. After decades of near continuous civil war, the government soldiers' hands were as bloodied as any rebels'. The troops were undisciplined, unpaid, and undertrained. They were a motley crew that protected no one in a country where pretty much everyone was vulnerable to violence. By 2006, it was decided that the United States would undertake the mission to transform them into a professional military. Today, Liberia's soldiers are among the best in the region. They have been vetted, trained, paid, and readied for action by the United States. To achieve this, the US Government spent more than $300 million to rebuild from this military from scratch. Every soldier admitted into the Army was vetted. The next batch of recruits for the AFL was just enlisted this year, and all 140 of them were put through a similar rigorous vetting. Since 2010, the US military has on average over 50 US military officers on the ground providing continuous mentorship and training for the AFL, yet as Commander, US Army Security Assistance Training Management Organization (SATMO), I was faced with delays in deploying trainers due incomplete vetting. COL Tim Mitchell, the current Defense Attaché still has to follow the requirements to validate and vet each individual AFL soldier prior to the arrival of a mobile training team or other training mechanism. This is time-consuming, bureaucratic, and unproductive, and has led on several occasions to AFL personnel not being allowed to receive the training. Despite these requirements, the same soldier can be "mentored" on an annual basis.

Leahy Law Ground Truths based on my professional experiences

(1) Credible allegations are all that is necessary to delay or prevent training

(2) Forces that fail to pass vetting usually are those forces most in need of external assistance to professionalize

(3) In-country vetting requires active cooperation from the client nation, and is seen in some cases, a direct infringement on national sovereignty

(4) Regional differences and insensitivities to differing local cultures still plague many countries in Sub-Saharan Africa.

(5) Many militaries are plagued the command and control infrastructure that does not allow its commanders in the field to have direct control of his forces.

STRATEGIC OPPORTUNITIES INTERNATIONAL

(6) Much of Africa is still developing a sense of national identity and that a sense of national patriotism would triumph over village, tribal, religious or regional affiliations in a time of crisis

(7) Engagement can equal access. Lack of engagement usually equals lack of access. We can't influence what we can't visit/see/assist/engage

Recommendations for improvements to the Leahy Law:

(1) Authorize DoD human rights training in a broad category of subjects similar to the expanded IMET program of the 1990's. Allow engagement that is designed to assist in the professionalization of those errant forces; focus on the law of land warfare, human rights, the military role in civil society and others similar subject.

(2) linked with Item #1 above, develop an exit strategy for bad individuals and units that will build toward the potential for full engagement. Rehabilitate and professionalize vice punish.

(3) Develop a blanket unit vetting process for forces free of violations.

In closing, I would like to remind everyone that if we don't engage, our global competitors can and usually will.

Mr. SMITH. Colonel Aubrey, thank you very much for your testimony. And coming from someone who actually was in the Embassy, provided this kind of training and vetting, it is very important that we receive your insights.

Colonel AUBREY. Thank you.

Mr. SMITH. We would like to hear from Mr. Rickard, if you could provide your testimony.

STATEMENT OF MR. STEPHEN RICKARD, DIRECTOR, WASHINGTON OFFICE, OPEN SOCIETY FOUNDATIONS

Mr. RICKARD. Thank you very much, Mr. Chairman, and thank you for holding the hearing. And thank you, Ranking Member Bass, and the other distinguished members of the committee for your commitment to human rights and to Africa, as demonstrated by your service on this important subcommittee. And I would be very happy to talk about some of the LGBT issues that the ranking member raised, which are extremely important.

I have worked on the Leahy law, in one form or another, for nearly 17 years. And I have discussed them with countless State Department and Defense officials, as well as human rights experts all over the globe. And the Leahy laws are just common sense. They prohibit the United States Government from arming and providing military training to security force or police units abroad that have been credibly alleged to commit a small list of the very worst human rights violations.

These laws do not prohibit the United States from providing assistance, even in the most violent conflict-wracked countries, like Nigeria and Colombia. On the contrary, because the Leahy law involves a unit-by-unit examination of human rights records, the Leahy laws provide a formula for the United States to engage in countries like Nigeria. They are a formula for success in those countries, not a prohibition on engagement.

Indeed, Colonel Aubrey's description of the success story in Liberia in his written testimony seems to me a perfect example of what can be accomplished when we build human rights vetting and training into our system from the ground up. If it can work in Liberia, and it can work in Colombia, it can work in Nigeria and elsewhere.

I would like the members of the committee to keep in mind four numbers when you think about the Leahy law. The first is 530,000. That is the number of units that the United States Government had considered training in just the last 3 years, 530,000.

The second number is 90 percent. That is the number of those units that got a quick response, a green light to proceed after they were vetted, generally within 10 days. There is even a fast track procedure for countries that have generally good human rights records.

The third number, which you referred to, Mr. Chairman, is 1 percent. Less than 1 percent of the time a unit is prohibited from receiving assistance under the Leahy law. It is not a burdensome requirement.

But the final number is 2,516. The Leahy law blocks aid in a tiny percentage of cases, but that doesn't mean it is unimportant. And 2,516 is the number of vetted units that the U.S. Government found to be credibly involved in gross atrocities in just the last 3 years.

In other words, without the Leahy laws, this hearing wouldn't be about a handful of units that DoD would like to work with but can't because of their atrocious human rights records; this would be a hearing about the 2,516 units that we did assist, that we gave guns to, that we gave military assistance to, and only later discovered that members of those units had committed murder, rape, and torture. The Leahy law stopped that, and it stopped it 2,516 times in just the last 3 years.

Those 2,516 units weren't being asked to meet a high standard. The Leahy law doesn't require pristine forces. The State Department defines gross human rights violations to cover five gross crimes: Murder, torture, rape, disappearances, and other gross violations of life and liberty. That is it. And the Leahy law doesn't even prohibit you from working with those units if the government will clean them up.

So when someone tells you that we can't work with a unit, I would encourage you to ask three questions. The first is, what did the unit do that got it on the list? If we can't work with them, it must mean that the United States has determined that that unit is one of the worst of the worst. It is in the 1 percent of units that the U.S. found credible information that they were committing murder, rape, torture, disappearances, or other gross crimes.

Second question: Why won't the government clean them up? The Leahy law lets you work with a unit if the government will take effective action. Maybe the government, as Colonel Aubrey has said, doesn't accept the U.S. commitment or it considers it an infringement on its sovereignty. Maybe it doesn't want to let the U.S. tell it what to do. Maybe the government has no control over the units, and it can't clean up the units, even if it wants to. But ask yourself: Why won't the government or can't the government clean up these units?

And finally; ask, if we know or believe that these units have committed the worst of the worst offenses, if the government will not or cannot clean up the units, why should the U.S. taxpayers pay to give those units, those specific units rather than other units, guns and military training?

There are a number of things that could be done to improve the Leahy law, and I think there is a lot of common ground here. We should increase funding for vetting. And I would note that since Colonel Aubrey's examples in Nigeria, there has already been a revolution in Leahy law vetting. An excellent database has been created. There are now 13 professional vetters who do this work. There is in fact a system to correct mistakes in the document. So there has been enormous progress in the last few years.

Two, we should make remediation and vetting a cost of doing business. We should set aside one penny out of every dollar to just say, ''This goes to vetting and fixing the bad units.'' If we want to be in Nigeria, that is just a cost of doing business there.

Three, we should train people. Many of the examples that Colonel Aubrey cites are examples of misunderstandings of the law. And if people had simply understood the law better, including the case that he cites in Uganda, that problem would have never arisen. So more training would be better.

In my written testimony, I respond to many of the common criticisms of the law, and I would be happy to do so in response to questions. But I would like to ask people to consider what the lower standard would be below the Leahy law. Should we take rape off the list of gross human rights violations? Should we take murder off the list? Should we say that if you haven't murdered anybody in 2 years, or 4 years, that is enough; now we will give you guns? Do we have a statute of limitations? This is the rock bottom human rights requirement that we should have.

Mr. Chairman, I am a preacher's kid, and the Bible tells us that—in the Book of Acts—before his conversion on the road to Damascus, the Apostle Paul was a persecutor of the Christian church. In fact, according to Acts, he was present at the killing at Saint Stephen, my namesake.

But the Bible tells us that he cast no stones himself at the killing of Saint Stephen. What he did was he held the cloaks of the people who did. He cast no stones, but he was complicit. He gave support to the people who did.

And when we go to places like Nigeria, shouldn't we at least ask ourselves, whose cloaks are we holding? Who are we handing stones to? That is what the Leahy law asks. That is all that it asks. Let us not be complicit in the worst human rights abuses in places like Nigeria.

Thank you, Mr. Chairman.

[The prepared statement of Mr. Rickard follows:]

Statement of Stephen Rickard

Executive Director
Open Society Policy Center

Presented to the
House Foreign Affairs Subcommittee
On Africa, Global Health, Global Human Rights and International Organizations

Human Rights Vetting: Nigeria and Beyond
July 10, 2014

I would like to begin by thanking Chairman Smith and Ranking Member Bass for holding this important hearing and for their leadership on human rights.

I have worked on the Leahy Laws in one form or another for nearly 17 years and have discussed them with countless State Department and Defense Department officials, as well as with human rights experts working all over the world. I also spent a period of time as a Franklin Fellow in the Department of State during which time I was able to learn in detail about the process for implementing the Leahy Laws. I have been engaged on detailed questions about the application of the Leahy Laws in Colombia, Turkey, Afghanistan, Sri Lanka, Indonesia, Nigeria, Kenya and dozens of other countries, and I believe that these laws are among the most important human rights statutes on the books. The law has been poorly funded – less than two-hundredths of one percent of the cost of U.S. military assistance is spent on Leahy Law vetting. And it has often been misunderstood and misrepresented.

But with President Obama proposing a new $5 billion fund for military assistance to combat terrorism it is essential to help the public understand this vital law and to help insure that it is vigorously implemented.

A Common Sense Formula for Security Cooperation Consistent With U.S. Values

The Leahy Laws are common sense laws that prohibit the United States Government from arming or providing military training to security force and police units abroad who have been credibly alleged to have committed gross human rights violations. These laws (there is one for State Department assistance and one for Department of Defense assistance) do not prohibit the United States from providing assistance in violent, conflict-wracked countries like Nigeria and Colombia. On the contrary, because they involve a unit by unit examination, the Leahy Laws provide a formula for the United States to assist foreign military forces even in countries where some government forces are committing gross atrocities. They are a formula for success in such countries, not a prohibition on engagement.

Four Numbers

There are four important numbers to keep in mind about the impact of the Leahy Laws. (All these statistics have been provided by the State Department and cover 2011-2013.) The first number is 530,000. That's the approximate number of foreign military and police units which the United States government considered arming or training over the last three years and subjected to Leahy vetting.

The second number is 90 percent. That is the minimum percentage of prompt approvals given under the Leahy Law – generally within 10 days of a request. There is even a "fast track" approval process for countries with generally good human rights records. Some vetting requests require more information, investigation or discussion. But at least 90% are approved more or less immediately.

The third number is 1 percent. In every one of the last three years less than 1 percent of all units vetted under the Leahy Law were ultimately declared to be ineligible for assistance under the law. Of course it is true that the number will be higher in some specific countries, but taken as a whole the Leahy Law actually blocks aid in a miniscule percentage of cases.

The final number is 2,516. The Leahy Law blocks aid in a tiny percentage of cases, but that doesn't mean that it is unimportant. Because the U.S. now provides training to so many people, even 1 percent is a lot. And 2,516 is the number of vetted units that the U.S. Government found to be credibly linked to gross atrocities over the last three years when it took the time to examine their records because of the Leahy Law.

Those 2,516 units were not being asked to satisfy a high standard. In no way does the Leahy Law require pristine forces. In fact, the State Department defines "gross human rights violations" to include a very short list of only the most heinous offenses: murder, torture, rape, disappearances and other gross violations of life and liberty. That's it. So even though less than 1 percent of proposed units failed the standard, it is still pretty shocking that over the last three years the United States Government probably would have armed and trained 2,516 units (or individuals in those units) containing murders, rapists and torturers without the Leahy Law.

The Leahy Laws don't actually prohibit the U.S. from working with even these units – the ones that have committed murder and torture. It only says that the U.S. cannot arm or train them *until the foreign government takes steps to clean up the unit.*

Three Questions

So whenever anyone says that it is a problem for the United States that it cannot train or arm a particular foreign battalion or police unit, one should ask three questions:

(1) What did the unit do? If we can't work with them, it must mean that the United States has determined that this unit is one of the worst of the worst. It is in the 1 percent of units where the U.S. government found credible information linking it to murder, rape, torture or another gross atrocity. So, when someone argues that we

should arm a Leahy-prohibited unit, one should ask, "What did the unit do to get on the list?"

(2) <u>Why won't the government clean up the unit</u>? Maybe the foreign government wants to make a point to the U.S. – it doesn't accept the U.S. commitment to human rights; it won't let the U.S. "tell it what to do." Maybe the government has no control over its own military and cannot do anything to clean up the unit even if it wanted to do so. But one should insist on knowing: "Why won't the government clean up the unit?"

(3) <u>Finally, if the unit committed murder, rape or torture and the foreign government won't or can't clean it up, why should U.S. taxpayers give that specific unit guns anyway</u>? Under what possible circumstances would it make sense for the United States to arm known killers who are either completely out of their government's control, or who work for a government that refuses to take any action against them?

<u>Responses to Three Criticisms</u>

Tempus Fugit: There are a number of arguments raised against the Leahy Law which might make some sense if the law covered lesser offenses. For instance, there is an argument that it makes no sense to keep a unit on the Leahy Law "pariah" list long after the atrocity occurred, especially if everyone who was in the unit has now moved on. But there are no other contexts in which we would accept a 4 year, or 8 year or even 15 year statute of limitations on murder, torture or rape. So why accept one here? And the law is intended to create an incentive for foreign governments to improve their human rights records and to hold people accountable. Letting a unit off the hook because the government rotated people out of the unit (and into other ones) or because the foreign government simply waited us out for a few years sends exactly the wrong message. Moreover, units have reputations and traditions that are regularly passed on to new members of the unit over many years and even decades. That is often true for units with gallant histories. But it is also true of death squads and praetorian guards.

Just as importantly, one needs to ask what it says about a foreign military "partner" if documented cases of murder, rape and torture go without redress after decades. The government always has the option of working with the United States to create new, carefully vetted units – something that has been done in a number of countries with gross human rights problems. If the government will not do that, it is probably trying to make a point. Is it appropriate to reward such behavior with assistance?

Pariah Forever: Critics of the law also sometimes argue that it is impossible for a tainted unit to be rehabilitated. This is, of course, completely false – unless the government in question refuses or is unable to take any meaningful action to address the problem. So what these critics are really saying is: It is almost never the case that America's military partners in these countries have the political will or commitment to human rights to take the kind of disciplinary action against killers and rapists that is absolutely routine in the U.S. military. And that is a very odd sort of argument for waiving or weakening the Leahy Law so that we can give more guns to these government's forces.

In fact, there are cases in which specific units have been rehabilitated. But it takes a willing partner. This is one area where critics of the law and its supporters should make common cause to support earmarked funding for remediation of tainted units. One percent of U.S. military assistance – just one penny out of every dollar – should be set aside for vetting and remediation. It should be used to help foreign militaries set up JAG officer corps, criminal investigation services and other elements of a professional disciplinary system. This should simply be considered a cost of doing business in some of the most violent places on earth. There is a precedent for applying a fixed surcharge as a "cost of doing business." Every time the United States Government sells weapons abroad it applies a surcharge – currently 3.5% – to administer the sale. The U.S. should apply a 1% surcharge to ensure that it knows what is being done with the other 99% and so that it can help move its partner forces in a positive direction on human rights.

Just a Few Bad Apples: Critics sometimes argue that it is wrong to hold whole units accountable for the acts of just a few, or perhaps even just one, member of the unit. They argue that we should vet specific individuals rather than units and only withhold information from those individuals who are linked to atrocities.

Here it is important to understand that the Leahy Law was a compromise. There was and is an important human rights law – Section 502B of the Foreign Assistance Act – which does not permit the United States to engage in a unit by unit assessment of foreign partner forces: "No security assistance may be provided to any country the government of which engages in a consistent pattern of gross violations of internationally recognized human rights." There is a very strong argument to be made under Section 502B that the United States *should be providing no assistance whatsoever to Nigerian forces, and many others around the world.*

But historically the United States has been extremely reluctant to invoke Section 502B even in the most extreme cases. So the Leahy Law was proposed as an intermediate step: If the U.S. will not completely cut off governments engaging in a consistent pattern of gross human rights violations, then *at least it should not arm the specific military units it believes are the ones actually committing the gross violations.* However, Senator Leahy also believed that it would be absurd and unreasonable to ask that human rights victims be able to identify the specific murder, torturer or rapist by name before the U.S. took any action. So, his law states that if credible information can be presented that links *an identifiable unit* to a specific atrocity the United States would be required to cut off that unit – at least until the foreign government identifies the specific individuals within it who are responsible and deals with them.

One Final Thought

The Bible tells us in the Book of Acts that before his conversion on the road to Damascus the Apostle Paul was a persecutor of the Christian Church. In fact, according to Acts (Chapter 7, Verse 59) he was present at the killing of St. Stephen and held the cloaks of those who stoned him. He cast no stones himself; but he was complicit. He gave aid to the killers. When we go to places like Nigeria, shouldn't we at least ask, "Whose cloaks are we holding?" That's all the Leahy Law says.

The Leahy Law cannot guarantee that the U.S. will never arm bad people. It's not a panacea. It's just the least we can do.

Attachment:

The Leahy Law by the Numbers

Number of "gross human rights violations" that trigger the law   5

Approximate dollars the U.S. provides in security assistance each year   15 billion

Number of countries receiving U.S. military training in 2012   158

Dollars directed to DRL Bureau in 2014 to conduct Leahy vetting   2.75 million

Leahy vetting costs as a percentage of U.S. military aid   .02

Number of Leahy vetters in DRL and regional bureaus   13

Approximate total number of Leahy vettings during 2011-13   530,000

Number of vetted units found to have probably committed gross atrocities 2011-13   2,516

Number of countries that had some aid withheld in 2011   46

Typical percentage of worldwide Leahy vettings that do not pass the vetting requirement   <1

Number of Leahy vettings carried out by U.S. mission in Abuja in 2012   1,377

Number of Nigerian military personnel rejected in 2012 due to human rights   211

Number of Nigerian military units currently vetted/cleared for security assistance   187

Number of prosecutions of Nigerian military officers for scorched earth assaults on civilians   0

Percentage added to the cost of a U.S. arms sale as an administrative fee   3.5

Percentage of U.S. military aid earmarked to help clean up bad units under the Leahy Law   0

Sources of Statistics in The Leahy Law by the Numbers

"....violations that trigger the law" - Derived from definition provided in Sec. 116 of Foreign Assistance Act

"Approximate dollars.....in security assistance each year" - State and Defense budget documents

"Number of countries...." - 2012-2013 Foreign Military Training Report

"Dollars directed to DRL...." - Line-item in FY2014 Omnibus spending bill report

"Number of Leahy vetters...." - Private communication from DRL staff

".....Leahy vettings in 2011" - State Department figure included in New York Times, June 21, 2013

"Number of units and individuals...." - Ibid.

"Number of countries...." - Ibid.

"Approximate number of Leahy vettings" - Senate testimony of Asst. Secretary of Defense Michael Lumpkin, March 11, 2014

"Typical percentage...." – *Statistics provided by the Bureau of Democracy, Human Rights and Labor and provided in Senate testimony by Secretary Clinton in answer to a written question from a hearing before the SFRC, February 28, 2012.* SOCOM Commander Adm. William McRaven gave a comparably small figure in Senate testimony on March 11, 2014 (about 2%)

"....US mission in Abuja..." - State Dept Inspector General Report of Embassy Abuja, February 2013

"....Nigerian military personnel rejected...." - Ibid.

"....Nigerian military units..." - Press release, Office of Senator Leahy, 28 May 2014

"....administrative fee" - Defense Security Cooperation Agency, Memorandum, September 17, 2012

Mr. SMITH. Mr. Rickard, thank you very much for your testimony.

We will take a short recess. There are a number of votes occurring on the floor. We have about a minute to get over and vote. So we stand in recess. Thank you.

[Recess.]

Mr. SMITH. The subcommittee will continue its hearing.

And Mr. Pittenger does have to go, but he would like to ask a question of the panelists, and then we will go to Ms. Massimino.

Mr. PITTENGER. Thank you. Really appreciate the good work that you all do, and certainly hope that our advocacy can make a difference for the lives of these wonderful people.

A motto I have lived by is inspect what you expect. So I would like to ask you, as we take a little bit more depth in the effectiveness of the Embassies, the DoD, and the State Department, and how they are doing in the vetting process. A fundamental piece of this discussion is knowing whether we are accurately identifying the good actors or if we are misidentifying bad actors as good ones. Ms. Blanchard, can we start with you?

Ms. BLANCHARD. That is a tough question. You know, the Embassies in many of these countries have to rely greatly on groups like Human Rights Watch and Amnesty International for the reporting. I mean, these Embassies are only staffed, particularly in Africa, by small staffs. So they are relying on that reporting, and then they have to determine whether that reporting is credible or not.

They also, you know, benefit from local journalists and local NGOs, and they have the very difficult task, particularly in countries like Nigeria that are strategically important, that face serious threats, in determining whether that information is valid on a security force unit or not.

So I think that, you know, there is a lot of challenge there. And when you have got short-staffed Embassies, it is——

Mr. PITTENGER. Sure. Makes a difference. Anybody else that would like to respond to that?

Ms. MARGON. I would be happy to make a quick response. I think the short answer is it depends. It varies very much from Embassy to Embassy. In some cases, it is particularly dependent on the Ambassador at the Embassy. We have seen a real overhaul in vetting in certain Embassies. I think the U.S. Embassy in Colombia has done a very good job of putting human rights vetting to the forefront of its relationship with the security forces there.

Doesn't mean the relationship is perfect. It doesn't mean the security forces themselves are perfect. In fact, they are quite the opposite still. But it has become a central part of the conversation, and each side knows what is expected.

The other piece that I would just add very briefly is that this is an important question because it is essential that the executive branch embrace the Leahy law and human rights vetting as part of its foreign policy, and so that they do a job both at the Foreign Service Institute in training officers but also encourage the military to train officers to understand the law, what it means to apply it, what the expectations are, and how to clean, if you will, units that have been dirty.

Mr. PITTENGER. Ms. Massimino?

Ms. MASSIMINO. Yes. I am so glad you asked that question, because there is another asset that we have or that we could exploit more fully in the Leahy vetting process, and that is, in addition to internationally focused NGOs, the local NGOs often have the best, most up to date, most reliable information, but a lot of times they don't understand how the process works, what level of detail they need, the form that the information needs to be in.

So it would be worth our while, I think, a good investment in reaching out, in having the Embassies reach out to those local human rights defenders, explain to them what the Leahy law is, solicit their information, develop relationships with them.

You know, the State Department has issued these human rights defender principles, guidance on how Embassies ought to interact with human rights activists in-country, and it really is kind of a blueprint for how to develop good relationships with those NGOs. And if those were fully implemented, I think we would have an additional resource in making sure that the vetting is well done.

Mr. PITTENGER. Thank you.

Colonel?

Colonel AUBREY. The only thing I would add to the discussion is the need to do a whole of Embassy approach on that, make sure that the defense attache is incorporated in there.

Part of the problem is, on the identification, is making sure that the units are properly identified. That DAT is going to know that the unit that came out of Sokuto that had this type of unit patch, that had this type of equipment that committed the violation was a particular unit.

And that way, even if the people reporting it don't understand the military order of battle, is that with a whole of Embassy approach—and you actually ask the accurate questions—it can actually be pinpointed properly.

Mr. PITTENGER. Thank you.

Mr. Chairman, I have one more question, if that is okay.

Mr. SMITH. Yes, it is.

Mr. PITTENGER. Thank you. Well, I would like to hear your thoughts on the real impact of the Leahy laws, that they have had. Do you feel that foreign countries have been impacted by our reluctance to aid security forces engaged in human rights violations? And, if so, could you give possible examples of what actions that they have taken?

Ms. BLANCHARD. In terms of effectiveness of the Leahy law, I think some of it depends on how much the country wants our assistance, and I think this may be a question in the case of Nigeria. In cases that want U.S. assistance, and there are a few on the continent that I think of as an example, countries like Colombia, if they want U.S. assistance, then they will generally comply with our rules and regulations.

And often you will see even senior military people switched out and units go through this process of remediation. And the clearer that the Embassy staff can be with the host country on how that remediation process works, the more likely we are to see accountability.

If a country doesn't want our assistance, then how effective can the vetting be? And that is——

Mr. PITTENGER. Sure. Thank you very much for your dedication and your good work.

And, Mr. Chairman, thank you for the courtesy——

Mr. SMITH. Thank you very much, Mr. Pittenger.

Mr. PITTENGER [continuing]. Of asking. I appreciate it.

Mr. SMITH. Ms. Massimino, if you could proceed.

STATEMENT OF MS. ELISA MASSIMINO, PRESIDENT AND CHIEF EXECUTIVE OFFICER, HUMAN RIGHTS FIRST

Ms. MASSIMINO. Thank you, Mr. Chairman. And thank you, members of the subcommittee. I appreciate the opportunity to be here today to share our views on human rights vetting and the critical role that it plays in advancing human rights and U.S. national security.

I want to also express my profound gratitude to you, Mr. Chairman, for your leadership on this and so many important human rights issues. You came to Congress about the same time that Human Rights First was born, and I feel like we have been working together ever since. There is really nobody in Congress, and very few people outside of Congress, who can match your passion and persistence. You are a constant reminder to your colleagues and to all of us that respect for human rights is not only the right to do; it is the smart thing to do.

And Human Rights First is actually an organization that is built on that idea. Our central mission is to foster American leadership on human rights, and human rights vetting requirements, the Leahy laws, are absolutely critical to that leadership.

When Secretary Kerry rolled out the human rights country reports this year, he said, ''The places where we face some of the greatest national security challenges today are also places where governments deny basic human rights to their nation's peoples, and that is no coincidence.''

As the U.S. expands its partnerships with foreign military and security forces to counter new threats, it is important to keep that in mind. Respect for human rights is neither a trump that beats other national interests, nor is it a soft concern that can be traded off or deferred without undermining those very interests.

Respect for human rights, rather, is the cornerstone. It is a foundation on which to advance other national priorities.

While the United States serves its national interest when it lives up to its ideals, the converse is also true. We have learned from years of experience that it is not just our reputation that is degraded when our partners engage in abusive and predatory practices; it is our security as well. Association with these abuses weakens U.S. moral authority, an increasingly, I think, undervalued resource these days, and alienates the civilian populations whose support is essential in the struggle against terrorism. And it is used by terrorists to validate grievances and to recruit others to their cause.

The Leahy laws are sometimes viewed as an insurance policy to minimize the risk that American leaders are seen as collaborators with criminals. And that is an important thing, but human rights vetting is much more than human rights risk insurance. I would like to focus on two other strategic objectives of the Leahy laws that underscore both its importance and its practicality.

First is the Leahy law's role in promoting accountability. In any country, real accountability in security services depends on the capacity and the willingness of civilian institutions to act. The Leahy laws encourage respect for human rights by providing an incentive for foreign governments to bring violators in their security forces to justice.

The Leahy laws by themselves can't ensure that our security partners will hold abusive individuals and units accountable. For the law to be effective, the U.S. must embed it in a broader human rights strategy. Proper training helps foster a culture of accountability, which is one of the reasons that professionalizing partner forces is a key component of our national defense strategy. Properly trained security forces understand the negative ramifications of human rights abuses, and, thus, are less likely to commit them.

So the vetting process required by the Leahy laws not only encourages the development of justice mechanisms, but when it is paired with robust training and assistance programs, it fosters professionalism with security forces that ultimately makes resort to those mechanisms less necessary.

The other strategic value of the Leahy laws is their contribution to the conduct of U.S. counterterrorism operations. By encouraging foreign governments to institute counterterrorism policies premised on the rule of law and respect for human rights, and by demanding accountability for human rights violations, the U.S. creates the legitimacy needed for effective counterterrorism operations and mitigates the conditions that help give rise to extremism.

Consider Colombia. The U.S. Embassy in Bogota has fully embraced the Leahy laws with two full-time staff positions dedicated to vetting 30,000 to 35,000 individuals annually. None of that was easy. It wasn't cheap, and Leahy vetting is not a panacea. But after a decade of effort and targeted aid that has spurred improvements, the Colombian Government continues to take action against many violators of human rights.

Finally, the Leahy law is just not an obstacle to pursuing our security goals. I know there are some, including in the military, and some here in the Congress, who have expressed concerns that the Leahy laws create an obstacle to our security goals because they bar the U.S. from equipping security forces on the front lines of conflicts, such as in Nigeria.

The logic behind this position is that in some conflicts there just are no good options, and that in service of a larger objective, against a bigger threat, the U.S. may need to tolerate units that have committed abuses.

But those concerns should be assuaged just by the facts. It is really important not to conflate the need to work with governments and militaries that have questionable human rights records with what the Leahy law is intended to prevent. For our part at Human Rights First, we believe that when the U.S. military interacts with foreign militaries, it is generally a net plus in terms of effectiveness, professionalism, and governance by the rule of law.

But no matter what lens you view it through, it is never in America's interest to arm or train or partner with individuals or units that are credibly believed to have committed torture, rape, or other such heinous crimes.

Now, I have heard, and I understand from the State Department and others, that the Leahy laws have never really prevented the U.S. from engaging in an essential operation. There has always been a more reliable, rights-respecting alternative.

As you heard from our colleague, Ms. Blanchard, the numbers really speak for themselves. If there is a problem getting training and assistance to the right people in Nigeria, I am not sure it is because of the Leahy laws. Clearly, we don't want the Leahy laws to end up disqualifying good people who share our goals and seek our support from getting it.

Those individuals are not covered under Leahy, and, in fact, it is not uncommon for a new unit to be created for the sole purpose of excluding abusers and making sure we can help those people who share our values and our goals. And not only should we be co-operating with those military forces who share our goals, we also should be working with them to help them demand accountability for those accused of crimes.

I suspect that the belief in some quarters that human rights vetting is a hindrance rather than a help in the country's battle against terrorism and other security threats might grow out of a failure to recognize its value. We all know that in the face of danger the big picture tends to get lost, and human rights vetting comes to seem a little bit like do-goodism that can be disregarded in the interest of national security.

But we should reject the temptation to cut moral and legal corners. The Leahy laws really derive from the bipartisan commitment to our country's ideals. And those ideals are a national security asset. And when we ally ourselves with those who undermine human rights, we are endangering ourselves.

Now, we have in the written statement several recommendations for improving implementation of the human rights vetting process, and maybe we can address those in the questions and answers.

But I thank you for your leadership, again, in holding this hearing, and for digging in as usual on the details of what can make human rights real.

[The prepared statement of Ms. Massimino follows:]

TESTIMONY OF ELISA MASSIMINO

PRESIDENT AND CHIEF EXECUTIVE OFFICER

HUMAN RIGHTS FIRST

HEARING ON

Human Rights Vetting: Nigeria and Beyond

Before the United States House of Representatives

Subcommittee on Africa, Global Human Rights, and International Organizations

July 10, 2014

Introduction

Thank you, Chairman Smith, Ranking Member Bass, and Members of the Subcommittee. I appreciate the opportunity to be here today to share our views on human rights vetting of potential recipients of U.S. security assistance and the critical role it plays in advancing human rights and U.S. national security.

We are grateful for your leadership, Mr. Chairman, on this and so many other important human rights issues. You came to Congress at about the same time that Human Rights First was born, and we've been working together ever since. No one in the Congress—and very few outside of it—can match your passion and persistence. You are a constant reminder to your colleagues that respect for human rights is not only the right thing to do; it's the smart thing, too.

Human Rights First, the organization it's my privilege to lead, is built on that idea. Our central mission is to foster American global leadership on human rights. We believe that upholding human rights is not only a moral obligation; it's a vital national interest. Our country is strongest when our policies and actions match our ideals. For 35 years, we have worked to ensure that the United States acts as a beacon on human rights in a world that sorely needs American leadership.

Human rights vetting requirements—known as the Leahy Laws—are absolutely critical to that leadership.

When Secretary of State John Kerry rolled out the State Department's Country Reports on Human Rights this year, he noted that, "The places where we face some of the greatest national security challenges today are also places where governments deny basic human rights to their nations' people, and that is no coincidence."

As the United States expands its partnerships with foreign military and security forces to counter new security threats—including terrorism—it's important to keep this in mind. Respect for human rights is neither a trump that beats other national interests, nor a "soft" concern that can be traded off or deferred without undermining those very interests. Respect for human rights is rather a cornerstone, a foundation on which to advance other national priorities.

While the United States serves its national interest when it lives up to ideals, the converse is also true: it is evident from years of experience that U.S. national security is degraded when our partners engage in abusive and predatory practices, as we've seen in many places, including Nigeria, Kenya, Colombia, and Iraq. Not only do such actions weaken U.S. moral authority—an increasingly under-valued resource—they alienate the civilian populations whose support is essential in the struggle against terrorism and are used by terrorists to validate grievances and recruit others to their cause.

The Leahy Laws prevent the United States from offering assistance to foreign military units if there is credible information that a member of the unit has committed a gross violation of human rights—torture, rape, murder, or indefinite arbitrary detention—and has not been investigated or held accountable. It is a common-sense proposition, a way to ensure that lethal aid only goes to law-abiding, responsible partners. It's not only one of the most constructive pieces of human rights legislation we have, it's an insurance policy. Because of the Leahy Laws, American leaders don't run the risk of being exposed as collaborators with criminals.

The Leahy Laws reduce the chances that the United States will become complicit in human rights violations by keeping lethal equipment out of the hands of those with a history of abuse. And having that conditionality enshrined in law sends an important message to potential partners and others that the United States will not support or condone such violations. Under the U.N. Charter and the International Covenant on Civil and Political Rights (ICCPR), the United States is obligated "to promote universal respect for, and observance of, human rights, and freedoms." The Leahy Laws help implement that obligation in a meaningful way.

I'd like to focus on two other strategic objectives of the Leahy Laws that underscore both its importance and its practical focus.

The Leahy Law Promotes Accountability

In any country, true accountability within security services depends on the capacity—and willingness—of civilian institutions to act. The Leahy Laws encourage respect for human rights by providing an incentive for foreign governments to bring violators in their security forces to justice.

The Leahy Laws set the standard. They establish in clear terms the professional, rights-respecting behavior the United States demands from its partners. But the law alone doesn't ensure that our security partners will hold abusive individuals and units accountable. For the law to be effective, the United States must embed it in a broader human rights strategy.

Proper training helps foster a culture of accountability, which is one of the reasons that professionalizing partner forces is a key component of our National Defense Strategy. Properly trained security forces will understand the negative ramifications of human rights abuses and will therefore be much less likely to commit them. Professionalism deters abuse. So the vetting process required by the Leahy Laws not only encourages the development of justice mechanisms, when paired with robust training and assistance programs it fosters professionalism within security forces that makes their reliance on those mechanisms a last resort.

In Bangladesh, for example, the United States carried out an interagency effort to assess the failure to investigate and prosecute human rights violations. The assessment focused on the Rapid Action Battalion, which was denied military assistance through the Leahy Laws because of clear evidence of human rights violations. The assessment represents a solid first step to instill professionalization and allows Leahy-prohibited units to overcome aid sanctions by holding abusers accountable.

The Leahy Law Promotes U.S. Security

The other strategic value of the Leahy Laws are their contribution to the conduct of U.S. counterterrorism operations. This is because upholding human rights and safeguarding security are complementary objectives.

By encouraging foreign governments to institute counterterrorism policies premised on the rule of law—and by demanding accountability for human rights violations—the United States creates the legitimacy needed for effective counterterrorism operations and mitigates the conditions that help give rise to violent extremism. To be sure, terrorists may attempt to harm U.S. interests regardless of our conduct but, because of the Leahy Laws, they are denied the public relations benefit. It's worth noting that Osama bin Laden cited United States support for regimes that violate human rights as a justification to attack us, calling the abusive governments "agents" of the United States.[1] Today, our largely unfettered aid to governments like Egypt is seen by many in the Middle East as approval of their abuses.

As stated by the U.N. Office of the High Commissioner for Human Rights, "effective counter-terrorism measures and the protection of human rights are complementary and mutually reinforcing objectives."[2] Human rights-compliant counterterrorism addresses both the short-term threat of terrorism and works to remedy the underlying conditions that give rise to terrorism.

Consider Colombia, where the Leahy Laws have resulted in an improved human rights climate and "gains in security and stability."[3] Testifying before Congress this year, Admiral McRaven cited Colombia as the best example of a country where U.S. military assistance and training have helped reform an abusive and ineffective foreign military. Indeed, the situation in Colombia—a society plagued by government corruption and conflict between the government and a violent insurgency—reflects the challenges in many of today's fragile states.

The U.S. Embassy in Bogotá has fully embraced the Leahy Laws, with two full-time staff positions dedicated to vetting 30,000 to 35,000 individuals annually.[4] None of this was

---

[1] Observer Worldview, "Full text: bin Laden's 'letter to America'" The Guardian, November, 24, 2002, *available at* http://www.theguardian.com/world/2002/nov/24/theobserver

[2] UN Office of the High Commissioner for Human Rights (OHCHR), *Fact Sheet No. 32, Human Rights, Terrorism and Counter-terrorism*, July 2008, No. 32, p. 19, *available at* http://www.refworld.org/docid/48733ebc2.html

[3] John J. Hamre, forward to Peter DeShazo, Johanna Mendelson Forman, Phillip McLean, *Countering Threats to Security and Stability in a Failing State: Lessons from Colombia* (Washington, D.C.: The CSI Press, 2009), p. v, *available at* http://csis.org/files/publication/090930_DeShazo_CounteringThreats_Web.pdf

[4] Nina M. Serafino et al., *"Leahy Law" Human Rights Provisions and Security Assistance: Issue Overview* (Washington, D.C.: CRS, 2014), p. 15. *available at* http://www.fas.org/sgp/crs/row/R43361.pdf

easy, and Leahy vetting is not a panacea. But a decade of effort and targeted aid have spurred improvements as the Colombian Government continues to take action against many violators of human rights.[5]

The Leahy Law is Not an Obstacle to Pursuing our Security Goals

Some—including in the military and the Congress—have expressed concerns that the Leahy Laws create an obstacle to our security goals because they bar the United States from equipping security forces on the frontlines of conflicts, such as in Nigeria. The logic behind this position is that in some conflicts there are no good options, and that, in service of a larger objective against a bigger threat, the United States may need to tolerate units that have committed abuses.

With all due respect, Mr. Chairman, this argument is wrong. Let's not conflate the need to work with governments and militaries that have questionable human rights records with what the Leahy Law is intended to prevent. No matter what lens you view it through, it is never in America's interest to arm or train or partner with individuals or units that are credibly believed to have committed torture, rape, or other such heinous crimes.

The problem isn't the Leahy Laws: the problem is security units that perpetrate and tolerate abuse. Human rights vetting is the tripwire that enables us to avoid arming them, training them, and—ultimately—undermining our strategic objectives. To blame human rights vetting is to blame the messenger of bad—and essential—news. The United States needs to know when security forces, because of their human rights records, do not have the trust of their own population. In the case of Nigeria, the abuses of some in the security forces have helped fuel the growth of Boko Haram.

In addition, as far as I understand from the State Department and well-placed Members of Congress, the Leahy Laws have never prevented the United States from engaging in an essential operation. There has always been a more reliable, rights-respecting alternative.

I also understand your credible concern, Mr. Chairman, that the Leahy Laws may end up wrongfully disqualify eligible soldiers—good people who share our goals and seek our support. Such individuals should not be covered under Leahy, and in fact, it is not uncommon for a new unit to be created with the sole purpose of excluding abusers. Not only should we cooperate with soldiers who share our goals, we should also be working with them to demand accountability for those accused of crimes.

I suspect that the belief in some quarters that human rights vetting is a hindrance rather than a help in the country's battle against terrorism and other security threats grows out of a failure to recognize its value. In the face of danger, the big picture gets lost, and human rights vetting comes to seem like do-goodism that can be disregarded in the

---

[5] Peter DeShazo, Johanna Medelson Forman, Phillip McLean, *Countering Threats to Security and Stability in a Failing State: Lessons from Colombia* (Washington, D.C.: The CSI Press, 2009), p. 42, *available at* http://csis.org/files/publication/090930_DeShazo_CounteringThreats_Web.pdf

interest of national security. But we should reject the temptation to cut moral and legal corners. The Leahy Laws derive from the bipartisan commitment to our country's ideals. We need to remember that those ideals are a vital national security asset, and that when we ally ourselves with those who undermine human rights, we endanger ourselves.

We have several recommendations for improving implementation of the human rights vetting process.

Recommendations

- **Unify the implementation and remediation guidelines**

    Full implementation of the Leahy Laws are impeded in part because there are two different provisions governing the Departments of State and Defense. The guidance to implement the Leahy Laws should be unified, and the process of remediation should be closely coordinated between the two departments.

- **Consider expanding the Leahy Laws to apply to intelligence agencies**

    As Americans know from our own history, abuse by intelligence agencies and officers is also possible, particularly given the lack of effective oversight of secret agencies in many societies. To strengthen the impact of Leahy Laws, Congress should consider expanding their reach to cover intelligence agencies.

- **Increase the numbers of vetters to expedite approvals**

    The State Department's Bureau of Democracy, Human Rights and Labor vets approximately 200,000 units and individuals per year. It has nine personnel in Washington and five globally dedicated to the task, supported by a point of contact in every embassy. In addition to investigating each name put forward for training, vetters also must verify the identity of the individual proposed for sanctions to avoid mixing up two people with the same name. The Treasury Department has an office of approximately 75 people assigned to this task. As Congress considers its FY15 appropriations, it should fund the Leahy vetting office at the level of $5 million contained in the Senate Foreign Operations and State Appropriations bill.

- **Expand the use of local activists in the vetting process**

    Human rights defenders, NGOs, and local activists in partner countries may have the most reliable information available for the accurate implementation of the law. But according to some embassy officials, they often lack an understanding about what kind of reporting and presentation the United States government deems specific enough to trigger a prohibition. The State Department should direct embassies to invest in better educating human rights defenders about the Leahy Law, the vetting process, and what role they can play to help it work the way it is supposed to work. Importantly, an investment in building defenders' capacity in this area would allow them to more effectively use the Leahy Law in their advocacy with their own governments as well.

- **Invest in Remediation Efforts**

Leahy vetting is a flag about the culture of accountability in a partner country. If a request for cooperation is denied, it is because credible evidence of a gross human rights violation has not been adequately investigated and prosecuted. One obstacle in remediating these cases is the lack of capacity to investigate, try, and discipline members of the military. Where the United States has an interest in partnering with countries that have challenges with accountability, it should be able to offer assistance to build this capacity. It is worth the investment, and indeed should be construed as the cost of doing business in lethal aid. In some cases, potential partners have been offered training through a human rights module from the Defense Institute for International Legal Studies (DILS). Courses such as these are generally inadequate to remediate the commission of the severe crimes Leahy vets. A stronger remediation effort would start with a human rights assessment conducted by the Bureau of Democracy, Human Rights, and Labor, and proceed to the design of a strategy focused on developing institutions that are central to accountability in the military and civilian sectors. The Administration should consider expanding programs in the Defense Department (such as the Defense Institute Reform Initiative, Ministry of Defense Advisors Program, and the Warsaw Initiative Fund), its supporting institutions (including the Center for Civil-Military Relations at the Naval Postgraduate School and the Army JAG school), and through US AID that train law enforcement and internal inspection units to properly respond to allegations of torture and abuse.

- **Exercise the "duty to inform"**

The Leahy Law includes a requirement to inform the host government of a denial of assistance because of a credible report of a violation. The State Department often chooses not to raise the denial with the host government for fear that it could complicate a bilateral relationship. In most cases, this is a missed opportunity to exert leadership on human rights. Without political attention, it is less likely that perpetrators will be held accountable or significant human rights training meant to assist in remediation will occur. Furthermore, a failure to inform obfuscates what the United States stands for and what it is -- and is not -- associated with. The United States should publicly embrace the Leahy Law, and the State Department should consistently inform host governments of its decisions on military training and justice and accountability.

- **The Leahy Law is critical to the success of any counter-terrorism partnership funding**

The President's request for the Overseas Contingency Operations includes $5 billion for a Counter-Terrorism Partnership Fund meant to provide resources to "build on existing tools and authorities to respond to a range of terrorist threats and crisis response scenarios." The request includes $4 billion to support capacity-building efforts to partner nations, among other purposes. Unfortunately, the request proposes that the Secretary of Defense use these funds "notwithstanding any limitation in a provision of law that would otherwise restrict the amount or recipients of such support or assistance." This appears to be designed to bypass the human rights vetting required by the Leahy Law in precisely the quarters it needs to be strengthened and made workable. Human Rights First urges Congress to strip this clause from any legislation funding counter-terrorism partnerships.

Thank you.

———————

Mr. SMITH. Ms. Massimino, thank you very much for your testimony, for your leadership for decades. And we will get to your recommendations as soon as we hear from our next witness, Ms. Margon.

STATEMENT OF MS. SARAH MARGON, WASHINGTON DIRECTOR, HUMAN RIGHTS WATCH

Ms. MARGON. Thank you. Mr. Chairman, thank you for inviting me to testify today. I am really pleased this subcommittee is looking at the details of human rights vetting and its application in Nigeria and beyond.

It is a timely hearing, given the impending U.S. redeployment from Afghanistan and the inevitable shift in resources and priorities that will occur. In fact, this shift has already begun with President Obama's recent creation of the Counterterrorism Partnership Fund and other correlated efforts to strengthen the capabilities of foreign military partners.

It is a renewed and expanded approach to security assistance that calls for reinvigorated attention to the Leahy law as a critical tool to finding the right balance between incentivizing institutional reform and addressing ongoing and systemic abuses that undermine larger U.S. security goals.

As you have noted, Mr. Chairman, the Leahy laws are an important means to ensure that the U.S. is not complicit in grave human rights abuses abroad, and that it upholds its international legal obligations. But it also makes sense within the larger foreign policy context, since militaries that commit abuses can also exacerbate longstanding grievances, escalate atrocities, foment political instability, and provide abusive armed opposition groups and terrorist organizations with a very powerful recruiting tool.

As examples, I would like to talk a little bit about our research in Nigeria, and then move off the continent for a second to talk about Iraq, given that it has returned to media pretty heavily.

Since long before the Chibok abductions, and the Bring Back Our Girls campaign captured the world's attention, Human Rights Watch has been reporting on the crisis in northern Nigeria and the serious abuses the security forces have perpetrated in responding to it. In 2009, we denounced the government's killing, while in custody, of Boko Haram leader Mohammed Yusuf and many others, acts which are widely believed to have spurned further violence by the group.

In October 2012, we released a report that looked not only at Boko Haram's atrocities, but also at the impact of Nigeria's heavy-handed security response. We found that in an attempt to halt increasing violent attacks between 2010 and 2012, Nigeria's security forces killed hundreds of Boko Haram suspects, along with members of local communities who were apparently attacked at random. Our research made clear that the members of the security force used excessive force, were physically abusive, detained suspects secretly, stole money, and burned homes.

In May 2013, Human Rights Watch issued another report examining massive destruction in the northern town of Baga. We used satellite imagery and witness evidence to confirm that while Boko Haram did attack a military patrol, kill a soldier, and wound five others, the government's response was directed at the local community, as government forces burned homes and killed local residents.

Our satellite images actually indicated high levels of building destruction, but because we were not able to visit the north we weren't able to confirm death figures from witnesses of almost 200 people.

Security force abuse in Nigeria is not limited to the Boko Haram crisis, as I am sure you know. It is deeply systemic. Over the years, we have documented many cases of abuse and apparent indiscriminate or excessive use of force outside of insurgency-related situations, from the oil-producing Niger Delta region, to arbitrary killings in response to intercommunal violence in Nigeria's middle belt, to political violence that often accompanies elections at all levels of government, to even small events such as one that occurred about a 1½ weeks ago in the city of Lagos, where it appeared soldiers went on a bus-burning rampage, randomly beating and harassing city residents after a bus ran over and killed one of their fellow fighters earlier that morning.

This abusive conduct completely undermines the security force's effectiveness and creates strong resentment within the communities they are ostensibly there to protect. In the case of Boko Haram, many Nigerians have expressed reluctance to share any information that might help stop the group, because they are afraid it will be used against them.

Worse still, the Nigerian Government has largely failed to undertake any kind of credible investigation in the ongoing and pervasive security force abuses that have repeatedly been brought to their attention. More than 10 years on, the government has still not held any members of the security forces accountable for a 2001 massacre of more than 200 people in Benue State.

If we turn to Iraq very briefly, as another example, where Prime Minister al-Maliki's heavy-handed approach to security has exacerbated security tensions, perpetuated impunity, and undermined the rule of law. We see that in January 2013, the Prime Minister promised to reform the criminal justice system, but a year later had done nothing and the brutal tactics of his security forces remain essentially the same.

In late May, just before the initial advance of ISIS, Human Rights Watch documented how Iraqi security forces were dropping barrel bombs on populated areas and attacking hospitals in Fallujah as the government intensified its campaign against a broadly defined group of insurgents.

This is not to say that Iraq hasn't been grappling with some very serious security threats. We know this. But the government's excessive use of force in law enforcement situations and violations of the laws of war has hindered rather than helped the country's counterterrorism efforts. He has terrified hundreds of civilians, killed thousands more, and the government has alienated affected populations, many of which could have been potential allies in the name of "combatting terrorism."

A cautious approach to security assistance, combined with robust Leahy vetting, is essential given the body of objective evidence in both cases implicating security forces in gross human rights abuses. The Washington Post editorial board noted earlier this week, if U.S.-backed forces commit human rights abuses, the damage is twofold. The fight against insurgents is compromised, and so is support for the alliance with the United States.

We also have a number of recommendations, which I will shorten, but very briefly the first is that Human Rights Watch would recommend support for the larger $5 million in the Senate appropriation for the Leahy vetting to ensure that Embassies have the right staff.

The second is for the administration, and Congress to press the administration, to move much more quickly on developing guidance for remediation and accountability.

And, finally, just to pick up on this last point that you mentioned earlier, the administration needs to do a much better job of publicly embracing the principles of the Leahy law at extremely senior levels and making clear both the implication and the consequences for all partner nations.

Thank you. I am happy to take your questions.

[The prepared statement of Ms. Margon follows:]

HRW.org

Testimony of Sarah Margon
Washington Director, Human Rights Watch

The House Foreign Affairs Subcommittee
on Africa, Global Health, Global Human Rights, and
International Organizations
July 10, 2014

"Human Rights Vetting: Nigeria and Beyond"

Mr. Chairman, Ranking Member Bass, and distinguished Members of the subcommittee, thank you for inviting me to testify today. I am very pleased this subcommittee is taking a closer look at human rights vetting, otherwise known as the "Leahy Law," and its application. I will focus my remarks today on what security force abuse actually looks like in Nigeria – and elsewhere – and why the Leahy Law is a key tool to address it.

This is a timely hearing given the impending US redeployment from Afghanistan and the inevitable shift in resources and priorities that will occur. In fact, this shift has already begun with President Obama's recent creation of a Counterterrorism Partnership Fund and other correlated efforts to strengthen the capabilities of foreign military partners. This renewed and expanded approach to security assistance reinvigorates the importance of the Leahy Law as it will be critical to find the right balance between incentivizing institutional reform and addressing ongoing and systematic abuses that undermine larger strategic US goals.

As you know, the Leahy Law was introduced by Senator Patrick Leahy in 1997 and prohibits US assistance to foreign security force units that the US government credibly believes have committed gross human rights violations. By restricting funds that many foreign governments would like to receive, it also serves as a lever to reform: security assistance can be restored to the offending unit when the partner government undertakes a credible investigation into the alleged abuses and begins a legitimate justice process.

In the grand scheme, the law is actually quite minimal – its baseline for not providing assistance is "gross violations of human rights" – which include crimes in violation of international law, including torture and other ill-treatment, extrajudicial killings, enforced disappearances, prolonged detention without charge, and politically motivated rape. There is no reason the United States should seek to affiliate with those who commit such egregious abuses.

In practice, there are only a small number of units that don't pass vetting annually. According to the State Department, in 2012, 90 percent of the 162,491 cases vetted were approved – only 1 percent was rejected and 9 percent suspended. In 2013, the percentages were about the same. These numbers make clear the Leahy Law isn't the obstacle some have portrayed it to be when it comes to providing security assistance.

Simply put, the Leahy Law is an important means to ensure that the US does not become complicit in grave human rights abuses abroad *and* that it upholds its international legal obligations. In and of itself, this would be a laudable goal. But it also makes sense within the larger foreign policy context since militaries that commit abuses can also exacerbate longstanding grievances, escalate atrocities, foment political instability, and provide abusive armed opposition groups and terrorist organizations with a very powerful recruiting tool.

Instead of pushing for waivers or looking to minimize the Leahy Law's reach, Congress and the administration should embrace the law and look for opportunities to strengthen and implement it robustly, within the context of broader governance and institutional reform. Such a path would uphold US moral and legal obligations while also contributing to the national security goal of supporting professional, accountable, and effective military partners – from Nigeria to Iraq.

I.   Nigerian security force abuses

Since long before the Chibok abductions and #Bringbackourgirls campaign captured the world's attention, Human Rights Watch has been reporting on the crisis in northern Nigeria, and the serious abuses the security forces have perpetrated in responding to it. In 2009, we denounced the government's killing, while in custody, of Boko Haram leader Mohammed Yusuf and many others, acts which are widely believed to have spurned further violence by the group.

In October 2012, we released a report that looked not only at Boko Haram's atrocities but also the impact of Nigeria's heavy-handed security response. We found that in an attempt to halt increasingly violent attacks, between 2010 and 2012, Nigeria's security forces – comprised of military, police, and intelligence personnel, known as the Joint Military Task Force (JTF) – killed hundreds of Boko Haram suspects along with members of the local communities who were apparently attacked at random. Our research made clear that members of the JTF used excessive force, were physically abusive, detained suspects secretly, stole money, and burned houses.

In May 2013, Human Rights Watch issued another report examining massive destruction to the northern town of Baga. We used satellite imagery and witness evidence to confirm that while Boko Haram did attack a military patrol, kill one soldier and wound five others, the government's response was directed at the local community as government forces burned homes and killed local residents. Nigerian officials claimed they only destroyed 30 homes but community leaders told us that immediately after the attack, they counted 2,000 burned homes and 183 bodies. Our satellite images actually indicated higher levels of building destruction but because we were not able to visit the north, we could not independently confirm the death figures.

Security force abuse in Nigeria is not limited to the Boko Haram crisis in the northern part of the country – it is deeply systemic. Over the years, we have documented many cases of abusive and apparently indiscriminate or excessive use of force outside of insurgency-related situations – from the oil-producing Niger Delta region to arbitrary killings in response to inter-communal violence in Nigeria's middle belt to political violence that often accompanies elections at all levels of government to smaller events such as one that occurred this July 4 in the city of Lagos, where it appears soldiers went on a bus-burning rampage, randomly beating and harassing city residents after a bus ran over and killed one of their fellow fighters earlier that morning.

The abusive conduct of Nigeria's security forces completely undermines their effectiveness and creates strong resentment within the communities they are ostensibly there to protect. In the case of Boko Haram, many Nigerians have expressed a reluctance to share any information that might help stop the group because they're afraid it will be used against them. Worse still, the Nigerian government has largely failed to undertake any kind of credible investigation into the ongoing and pervasive security force abuses that have been repeatedly brought to their attention – a problem that only aggravates the underlying governance problems that enable groups like Boko Haram to thrive. More than 10 years on, the government has still not held members of the security forces accountable for the 2001 massacre of more than 200 people in Benue State.

Ultimately, the Chibok kidnappings have made clear to the world that Nigeria is confronted with a major security challenge where military action alone will not solve the problem. Similarly, the Leahy Law is not a panacea that can "fix" the Nigerian security forces but it can play a crucial and positive role in helping the Nigerian government take steps to reform their security forces so down the road the US can engage more extensively.

II.   Other security force abuses

As you well know, abusive and undisciplined security forces are not unique to Nigeria. They are a problem in many countries where corruption is widespread and governance is weak. Notably, these are also some of the conditions that give rise to or allow violent extremism to thrive.

One example is Kenya, where over the past five years the police have been responsible for hundreds of extrajudicial killings, torture, and other gross human rights violations. Kenyan authorities did prosecute about six people associated with the 2007-2008 post-election violence that nearly plunged the country into a protracted conflict. But compared to the 5,000 case files that were collected in 2011 by the Director of Public Prosecutions to review, it has barely made a dent. As a result, underlying concerns that led to the violence remain unaddressed, as do many of the surface level tensions.

Kenyan police, in particular its Anti-Terrorism Police Unit (ATPU), have also been implicated in dozens of cases of extrajudicial killing, enforced disappearance, and torture of terrorism suspects in Nairobi and the Coast in recent years.

In addition, Kenyan police and security authorities, including the ATPU, have cracked down harshly on ethnic Somali Kenyans and Somali refugees in large-scale, abusive operations, notably in Eastleigh in operations in 2012-2013 and 2014. In interview after interview, Human Rights Watch learned how the police enter homes, steal money, arbitrarily detain people in horrible, degrading conditions and then threaten to charge them – without any evidence – of terrorism.

Human Rights Watch has also documented police and military abuses against Somali Kenyans and Somali refugees in the former North Eastern Province, where police regularly intercepted thousands of asylum seekers, mostly women and children, fleeing conflict in Somalia and beat, raped, and/or deported or detained those who could not pay bribes on false charges of unlawful presence in Kenya. In 2012, police and military personnel took part in roundups and beatings of civilians in the northeastern city of Mandera.

Another example is Iraq, where Prime Minister Nouri al-Maliki's heavy-handed approach to security has exacerbated sectarian tensions, perpetuated impunity, and undermined the rule of law. In January 2013, the prime minister promised to reform the criminal justice system, but a year later nothing had been done and the brutal tactics of his security forces remained essentially the same. In late May – just before the initial advance of the Islamic State of Iraq and Sham (ISIS) – Human Rights Watch documented how Iraqi security forces were dropping barrel bombs on populated areas and attacking hospitals in Fallujah as the government intensified its campaign against a broadly defined group of insurgents. This is not to say that Iraq hasn't been grappling with some very serious threats. Unfortunately, the government's excessive use of force in law enforcement situations and violations of the laws of war hindered, rather than helped, the country's counterterrorism efforts. By killing hundreds of civilians and terrifying thousands more, the government alienated affected populations – many of which constituted potential allies – in the name of "combatting terrorism." Aggressive discrimination by government officials, state security forces, and the Shia militias they have been working alongside for the past several years has polarized the population and amplified sectarian tensions. Such unlawful tactics do little to reduce violence but instead may make the situation worse. It comes as no surprise to many experts that despite their numerous horrific abuses, ISIS has been able to advance so quickly in Iraq.

In both of these examples, a cautious approach to security assistance combined with robust Leahy vetting is essential given the body of objective evidence implicating security forces in gross human rights abuses. Otherwise, as the *Washington Post* editorial board wrote earlier this week, "if US-backed forces commit human rights abuses, the damage is twofold: the fight against insurgents is compromised, and so is support for alliance with the United States."

Recommendations
In the nearly 20 years since the Leahy Law became law and as the administration places greater emphasis on building the capacity of foreign security forces, it is entirely appropriate for the administration and Congress to explore how to make improvements so the law can be more effective. Specifically, we are concerned that human rights vetting remains deeply underfunded, that many within the US government, as well as other governments, don't understand the law or its implications, and that the executive branch hasn't provided sufficient policy guidance on steps other governments can take to address problems of abuse within their security forces.

To that end, Human Rights Watch would like to recommend a few steps forward.

First, Congress should appropriate sufficient funds to support the Leahy vetting process. Currently, the US government vets approximately $15 billion of US security assistance (between State Department and Defense Department funded aid) annually. The FY15 House Foreign Operations Appropriations includes $2.75 million appropriated in support of the Leahy Law while the Senate version increases the amount to $5 million. Human Rights Watch urges you to support the Senate amount, as increased funds are crucial to support staffing and computer infrastructure in Washington. In key embassies around the globe – where vetting begins – these funds will help expedite and strengthen the process.

Second, Congress should press the administration to develop clear policy guidance on how diplomats and military officials can support foreign governments to promote accountability for abuses committed by foreign security forces. The Leahy Law requires the administration to offer assistance in remediation, but this area of the law and associated policy are woefully underdeveloped. In some countries, such as Colombia and Bangladesh, there have been efforts to support an attempt to clean up the abusive units unable to receive funds, but this approach is all too rare. The US government should build out this central tenet of the Leahy Law by capitalizing on the wide-ranging in-house expertise on developing and supporting judicial mechanisms for accountability and the rule of law.

Finally, the administration should publicly embrace the principles of the Leahy Law by clearly and transparently communicating its requirements and consequences to all partner nations. As a law reaching beyond US borders, US ambassadors and their staff need to understand the law's implications, explain it to foreign governments, and clarify what assistance could be available if they reform abusive units. This will entail publicly articulating which units are barred from receiving US security assistance, why, and precisely what reform efforts a government must undertake to reverse the ban. Doing this would make a positive and lasting contribution to accountability and the rule of law by showing US commitment to upholding and improving respect for international human rights, and expecting its partners to do the same.

Thank you Mr. Chairman. I'm happy to answer your questions.

Mr. SMITH. Thank you very much for your testimony, and for your specific recommendations, which will be very helpful to the subcommittee.

All of your comments and testimony I think will be of tremendous nature. We are in an inflection point. We are at a crossroads, I think, especially with the President's proposal and the language that you, Ms. Blanchard, pointed out in a June 26 submission to Congress with regards—that would seemingly bypass the Leahy amendment, the ''notwithstanding'' language, any limitation in the provision of law that would otherwise restrict the amount or recipients of such support or assistance, contingent on notification to Congress that it is in the national security interest to do so, as part of the Counterterrorism Partnership Fund. And I thank you for amplifying that in your testimony.

So this does come I think at an important point in this debate. I would like to ask one general question about Nigeria, and, Colonel Aubrey, you might want to be first to answer it. We tried as a committee for approximately 2 years to get the administration to designate Boko Haram a foreign terrorist organization.

Matter of fact, Greg Simpkins and I traveled to Jos and to Abuja last September, and the primary reason for going was to try to figure out why that FTO designation was not forthcoming, which, again, just like Leahy is not a panacea, nor is FTO, there is no panaceas, but there are tools in the toolbox that could help choke and stop the flow of funds, or at least figure out where those funds are coming from. And sooner is always better than later, rather than waiting to a Stage 4 cancer, which Boko Haram has become.

And so my question is, when we get to training properly vetted, Mr. Rickard talked about 530,000 as the number, and you have a number of different periods, Ms. Blanchard, in your testimony—but large numbers of troops, service members, have been trained pursuant to Leahy. Only a small percentage are excluded. It does take some time, of course.

But the question would be about the small number, the infinitesimal small number, of Nigerians who indeed have been trained, especially since Mr. Jackson had testified on the Senate side that roughly half of the Nigerian forces would be eligible for military training. And that is especially important in counterinsurgency training.

So your thoughts on, you know, 1,200, 1,300, I don't know what the number is for Fiscal Year 2013. But it is not much when one battalion is trained and, you know, the need for five to ten with that very special skill-set, human rights-oriented. Your thoughts on that. It seems like it is too small.

Colonel AUBREY. I am not sure that numbers itself really is relevant on that. I have always felt that the Nigerian Army had sufficient strength to protect its borders. What you are talking about is national will, Chairman, is do they have the wherewithal and do they have the trust of their military to effectively train and arm and deploy. And I say that, you know, very cognizant about their military history.

While I was present in Nigeria, we were very confident that the amount of ammunition that they would issue out their soldiers was usually zero, that we had people going through training in Jaji, the

Infantry Training Center, preparing to deploy to Darfur that had been in their unit for 5 years and had never fired their weapon once.

It is incumbent on the National Command Authority to trust its elements of defense and security. Unfortunately, the history in Nigeria does not lend the civil administration great confidence of that. And that is why my—my current military peers that had served in the 1990s probably will curse me for my statement about expanded IMET.

I know that when I had to implement that I was not happy about having to do some of the Defense Sector Reform initiatives prior to doing regular military training, because that is what, you know, the targeted nation wanted. But there is something to be said about teaching a military's proper role in civil society, both on the civilian side where the civilians understand how to properly command and control the military, but having the military understand the divisions.

In Nigeria, the incidences that have been talked about, that is their own people that they are going into, that it is not enemy combatants on a foreign shore. So understanding that civil-military relationship, taking some of the lessons-learned that we have learned from 13 years of combat in Afghanistan and Iraq, and how atrocities make the jobs more difficult. It makes achievement of the mission goals much more hard.

You know, I don't have a solution. Just an observation that, you know, the problem in Nigeria is trust.

Mr. SMITH. Yes.

Ms. BLANCHARD. I think Colonel Aubrey has touched on a number of the issues. I think there is certainly an issue of political will, and also of follow-through on the part of the Nigerians.

If you look at the two areas of security cooperation where we have had the most success, it has been in peacekeeping training and in maritime security and counternarcotics. The Nigerians have recently been making the decision to scale back their contributions to peacekeeping, and they are dropping further down the list. And they were always one of the top five contributors. They are no longer. So they are making some different decisions about how they allocate their military resources.

In terms of special forces capabilities, they haven't prioritized that. We started, I believe, in 2010 to try to work with a special counterterrorism unit. They didn't keep the unit together. We are facing that challenge now where they are still debating whether a unit that has been cleared and trained to do counterterrorism missions will actually have that mission.

So there have been some challenges I think in follow-through, particularly in engagement with us on things that we have offered and things that they have taken us up on. So I will leave that.

Mr. SMITH. Yes.

Ms. MARGON. Just wanted to pick up on those points. I think you raised the right question. And in the grand scheme, the small number of units that have been trained are not enough, but it is important to remember a couple of things.

First is in the specific case of Boko Haram, a military solution is not going to fix the problem. And so while it may be that more clean units need to be engaged, it is not solely a military problem. It needs to be engaged in a much wider and more comprehensive approach, which requires much greater political will from the government in Abuja. That is the first point.

The second point——

Mr. SMITH. On that point, if I could——

Ms. MARGON. Sure.

Mr. SMITH [continuing]. Is it possible that Boko Haram has gotten to the point where—I mean, we are looking at ISIS every day and seeing the gains they are making in Iraq, which seems to have caught many people flat-footed, both in Baghdad as well as in Washington and other capitals.

They have built up a critical mass. They weren't supposed to be able to project power on Abuja, and a month before we got there they blew up a bus station. It is almost as if they are extending with impunity their ability to kill and maim, and of course the Chibok schoolgirls' abduction, followed by other abductions, and slaughter of young men as well, and boys, in school. It is as if the terror reign has gone to an unprecedented level, and they have gotten stronger, not weaker.

So just a thought, but your thoughts on that.

Ms. MARGON. Yes. I wouldn't disagree. I think we have reached a much more violent and expanded version of Boko Haram right now. I do think in part that has to do with the heavy-handed approach from the Nigerian security forces in their response, not exclusively, but I do think over the short term what the Nigerians need to be looking at is putting together units and putting political will behind that to deal with the immediate military and protection concerns.

But then there are also needs to be a much larger response that looks at the historical marginalization and disenfranchisement and poverty of the north that has enabled Boko Haram to capitalize on and move forward with that type of strategy.

Mr. SMITH. Yes. Ms. Massimino?

Ms. MASSIMINO. I would just reinforce what Colonel Aubrey said, because I thought really you crystallized the problem that is often faced with human rights vetting and with so many other situations where we are faced with kind of a short-term/long-term—you know, what appears to be a conflict.

And I really welcomed your comment that, you know, this is not—doesn't feel as urgent perhaps to establish these mechanisms for accountability, buildup, you know, foreign military's JAG corps, educate them about the proper relationships with their civilian masters, and all of that. But if we don't do that, everything else is harder. And so holding to the discipline of that is really important, and I think that is exactly what we are facing with implementation of the Leahy laws.

Mr. SMITH. Ms. Margon, you have mentioned in your testimony, in your recommendations section, that Congress should press the administration to develop clear policy guidance on how the diplomats and military officials can support foreign governments, promote accountability.

And you also point out, ''Finally, the administration should publicly embrace the principles of the Leahy law.'' Especially with regards to Nigeria, has that happened at the highest levels of our Government?

Ms. MARGON. I would say that in the aftermath of the Bring Back Our Girls campaign, there has been a very clear understanding at senior levels from this Government, from this administration, about the need to be cautious in engaging with the Nigerian military. The administration is well aware of the problems.

Has it been embraced prior to that? Not in the way that it should have been. It doesn't mean that any laws are being violated. Of course not. But it does mean that engagement at the Ambassador level and at the Embassy needs to be much more robust when U.S. Government officials, particularly military officials, are going to Nigeria, human rights vetting and security cooperation needs to be a top talking point, which, to the best of my knowledge, it has not been until very recently.

Mr. SMITH. Has it been enough of a priority—and, Colonel, you might want to speak to this as well—within the administration to say Boko Haram is a lethal growing cancer on the body politic of Nigeria? Just like al-Shabaab did such unbelievable damage, still does, in Somalia and now is projecting that damage to Nigeria, to Kenya, and elsewhere.

My feeling is, and you don't have to share it, is that there has been an underappreciation of the threat, which means we could have been accelerating the number. If half of the Nigerian military is eligible to be trained, by implication that half are not, pursuant to Leahy, why aren't we training more, and why is there not a hurry-up offense to get as many well-vetted but specially trained troops to protect the Nigerian people, the largest country in sub-Saharan Africa?

Ms. BLANCHARD. If I could speak to that.

Mr. SMITH. Please do.

Ms. BLANCHARD. The administration I think has taken very seriously the threat posed by Boko Haram for quite a long time. I think one of the challenges—and former Assistant Secretary Carson made it clear that one of the reasons that the deliberations on whether or not to designate Boko Haram a foreign terrorist organization took a while, was that there was concern raised by a number of NGOs and African studies academics here in the United States and elsewhere about actually labeling the group a foreign terrorist organization.

Now, the State Department made several statements labeling them a terrorist organization, but on the actual FTO designation. The concern was that that might be seen to give a green light to the security force abuses that they were seeing in the northeast by the Joint Task Force. Those reports went back, obviously, to what Sarah talked about back to 2009.

But particularly as the Joint Task Force stood up, from 2011 onward, we were seeing a lot of very, very serious reporting coming out, and there was the concern that the Nigerian Government might perceive that designation to give a green light to those operations.

And on the flip side, there was not clear evidence, from what I understand from talking to administration officials, that the implications of the FTO designation, i.e. the ability to freeze funds in the United States and stop travel of Boko Haram individuals in the United States, would have much of an effect. There wasn't evidence to suggest that there was a lot of——

Mr. SMITH. Well, I get your point, but there is a larger issue whether or not sufficient personnel are deployed at Treasury, for example, even now, that FTO has been so designated to really make a difference and to work this 24/7 to try to find out where the AK–47s, the IEDs, and everything else is coming from. And I have asked those questions, and I have not gotten the kinds of answers that would make one sleep well at night.

We are not working it, in my opinion, the way we could or should. That is even FTO. So I just throw that out. Anybody else want to comment on the issue?

Colonel AUBREY. Mr. Chairman, the only thing I would add is that the extremist issue in the trans-Sahel area is not a new one, and it isn't a new one to the Department of State, to Congress, or to the Department of Defense.

I go back to where I sit on national will. Burkina Faso for years denied that there were issues in the north, and it was only after many years and many discussions that they actually acknowledged. The host nation has to request the assistance, you know. And until they do, until they recognize the problem, it is hard to help a partner nation develop an effective strategy.

Mr. SMITH. Let me just ask the question with regards to units versus individuals and just get each of, if you would, your thoughts on that. You make the point, Colonel, that sometimes the taint is forever. And I was talking to Elisa Massimino before we reconvened, and it just struck me that there are a number of units in the U.S. military, including the unit that Lieutenant William Calley was a part of, the Abu Ghraib deployment, where the bad apples were prosecuted. Not enough, obviously, with Lieutenant Calley; he is the only one who was convicted as a result of the My Lai massacre in Vietnam.

And it just seems to me that maybe reconstituting or encouraging host governments like—or friendly governments like Nigeria to come up with a brand-new unit, as opposed to an old unit that has a terrible reputation.

And as you point out, Ms. Blanchard, you know, there is a tension there, and you do quote Admiral William McRaven in Congressional testimony that while he supported the vetting process, it has restricted us to the number of countries and our ability to train units that we think need to be trained. Individuals—that is an absolute, that individuals should be vetted to the greatest extent possible.

But it does become at least problematic about the unit side. Your thoughts on that, because it seems to me that it is worth a discussion, and I am sure there will be a little difference of opinion as a panel.

Colonel AUBREY. And I will bring myself back to my—what had been my profession for most of my adult life, is we are quite proud of those little pieces of cloth, the streamers that hang from our regimental colors, and so forth. Asking someone to rebadge doesn't usually sit very well with a soldier. They are quite proud of their unit lineage.

If you look at the battle streamers on the Army colors, they date back to Valley Forge. So approaching any other country's units to discuss, you know, reconstitution doesn't necessarily sit well. Whether or not we agree with their lineage, a lot of times they are quite proud of their lineage. That on these units they—you know, because of their colonial past, they talk about the colonial wars they fought, or what they did in the First World War, the Second World War, and are quite proud, and rightfully so, of their lineage.

I think what is even more important is that for the Leahy vetters, whether it is in the Embassy or with INVEST, is that they understand the order of battle, and understand what the units really mean. What is the difference between a section or a platoon, a division, a battalion? Who ranks what, the sergeant or the general? And that would be effectively—to understand what the unit rotation is, what is the turn of enlistment to the unit?

Liberia, which had a turn of enlistment, they just—the first batch of—they have just brought in their second batch of recruits since the LAF was reconstituted. So if you know that they are going to do a rotation in 6 years, that if a unit had done something 10 years ago, the chances of anybody being in that unit, having committed that atrocity, is gone.

That would be much more effective than saying take the 131 that committed atrocities in Maiduguri 3 years ago, and we are going to rebatch it as the 151, because we won't know.

Mr. SMITH. Thank you.

Ms. Massimino?

Ms. MASSIMINO. Yes. So the examples that you gave of U.S. units, where there were abuses, you know, those are examples where there was investigation, prosecution, and I think in order to get the full value of the Leahy laws and human rights vetting, as I said in my testimony, you don't want that viewed in sort of a narrow way where you just kind of rearrange the deck chairs and see if you can assemble.

I mean, that is one way, and it is perfectly permissible under the law to create new units and all that. But, really, what we want, what we all want, fundamentally, the Leahy law is to prompt better human rights performance, stronger commitment on the part of the militaries and the governments to accountability and the rule of law. And you don't get that if you are, you know, just rearranging the deck chairs.

But, you know, as to these units that, you know, have this sense of identity and cohesion and all of that, there is nothing inherently wrong with that. But we all know that there are units that are, you know, proud and have cohesion around the wrong things. They are notorious for being human rights violators.

And I think there you really have to wonder whether long term the interests are going to be served if you are balancing those interests with keeping that band of brothers together when what has drawn them together and the identity of the unit is not something you want to perpetuate.

Mr. SMITH. Yes.

Ms. MARGON. Just quickly, I think if you are talking about rogue elements or abusive units within an otherwise law abiding military in the country, then the units should be disbanded and prosecuted, the individuals should be prosecuted. This is in fact what we have recommended in specific cases in Bangladesh, Indonesia, and Afghanistan. But if it goes beyond the rogue elements or the abusive units and is a more endemic problem within the security forces, then nothing else is going to suffice, as Elisa said, when it—as opposed to accountability or prosecution.

And there the U.S. can plan a really important role. The State Department, USAID, Defense Department, and Justice all have really deep and varied experience in helping set up justice mechanisms, technical expertise. Prosecution is a critical component that helps with the institutional reform, so it really depends on what you are looking at when it comes to the unit.

Mr. SMITH. Let me ask—oh, yes. Ms. Blanchard?

Ms. BLANCHARD. Just a final point. Three things. I think, one, creating new units demonstrates political will, and we have seen a number of important security partners on the continent that do that, because there are issues with tainted units, and we have been able to move forward, particularly contributors to the mission in Somalia.

A second point is that the vetting process should really ensure that they try to identify the smallest unit possible when they have evidence of an abuse. We have seen cases in important security partners, again, in East Africa, where larger units have been tainted because the NGO reporting on the information wasn't able to get it down. And as a result, we have had important counterterrorism training postponed with very key battalions.

And then, the third point is the fact that there are differences in the laws, and perhaps there are differences in the laws for a reason. The State Department/FAA Leahy provision requires that these individuals be taken to justice. The language in the DoD law is slightly different, and, as a result, you can have the individual taken out and not necessarily go through a court of law system to get the unit back to being eligible for training.

Mr. SMITH. I have a lot of other questions. I will ask them all and ask of you, whichever ones you would want to respond to.

First, starting with—I went on the Web site for the Nigerian Army last night, and one of the feature parts of that Web site talks about how the International Committee for the Red Cross is collaborating with the NA, the Nigerian Army, and it talks about a training the trainers program, law of armed conflict programs. Obviously, I think they are primarily focused on peacekeeping, but I guess they might be talking about other good human rights-oriented behavior.

What is your thought on that kind of collaboration? Because obviously it is front and center, and hopefully, you know, the ICRC is conveying some very important principles and best practices with regards to human rights.

Secondly, some of you may know that I am the prime author of the Trafficking Victims Protection Act of 2000. When we did the reauthorization in 2003, we added a provision that militaries would be part of the minimum standards, and I still am concerned that when we look at a country's performance vis-à-vis the minimum standards prescribed in the law, that militaries are not sufficiently taken into consideration as to the tier ranking, Tier 1, Tier 2, Tier 3, or Tier 2 Watch List.

And I am wondering, with regards to Leahy, how focused are we on trafficking with regards to a military? I have tried unsuccessfully for well over a decade to establish an Assistant Secretary within DoD's chain of command that would be focused at an office exclusively on trafficking, because I am great believer because I talk to generals and armed forces leaders throughout the world every time I travel it seems. I always bring up trafficking, and when a politician or a lawmaker brings it up, it certainly does not have the gravitas that it would have if a colonel or somebody with a few stars was talking military to military, training the trainer, so to speak, language.

I know that DoD does a wonderful job in many cases, but I am wondering if in the vetting process trafficking, particularly sex trafficking, is included. And we know of the things that Shekau said was that he was going to sell the women from the Chibok school, and the young girls. No one knows if that has happened, but obviously trafficking is everywhere, and it is a horrific crime.

Thirdly would be, if somebody is unfairly excluded, say a commander has a platoon or a squad, a number of people that, really, are up and comers, they really are wonderful soldiers, and somehow they get excluded in the vetting process, or not enough information is known, what does happen with those people? Do they get a second chance?

Is there an appeal process to—because obviously upward mobility even, but also capability in terms of fighting a group like Boko Haram is enhanced if your best soldiers are included, and they are also human rights-vetted. So the appeals process would be another question.

Also, delays. You mentioned, Colonel, that when you were a commander, U.S. Army Security Systems Training Management Organization (SATMO), "I was faced with delays in deploying trainers due to incomplete vetting." If you could maybe—and others, if you would like, but if you could expand upon, what kind of delays are we talking about? Is it a week, a month? Is it forever for some? How does that work in terms of your ability to match up a trainer with a group of soldiers that are in need of that training?

And the INVEST program, Ms. Margon, your point about the $5 million being far superior than the just under $3 million for the vetting process, and 13 people I think is the number that are at DRL. How important is that? Is that really a make or break issue? All of you might want to speak to that, but it seems to me that if you don't have the personnel deployed, the job doesn't get done.

I know in our Embassy in Nigeria we do have—and I actually watched a vetting process happen with the Google search and INVEST, and it was one they had already done, but it was just to show me how, because I had never seen it actually done, at least at that stage.

Is there room for improvement there? Is the INVEST program database accurate? Is it something that needs improvement, or is it just a work in progress, always going from good to getting better?

So there are a couple of questions. And, again, you might want to touch on those policy tensions that, Ms. Blanchard, you have talked about, between the military and state and human rights community, which can be benign tensions. Everyone is looking out for—or hopefully striving for the same ultimate goal here, but we need to learn from each other.

But if you could perhaps address some of those questions.

Ms. BLANCHARD. I will start with the first issue you raised, the Nigerian Army engaging with the ICRC, and I think that is a great development if it is happening. I think one of the trends that we see, not just in Nigeria but in countries like Kenya and elsewhere where you have security force abuses, they often can be linked to breakdowns in the criminal justice system. You see frustration from local police, from the military, that individuals, you know, be they Boko Haram or otherwise, are not going through the system.

And, as a result, particularly in Nigeria, we have seen massive detentions. These are not criminal justice detentions, but you are seeing thousands of people held in military facilities, particularly in the northeast, in Borno, in horrific conditions. So if ICRC can engage with the Nigerian military on how to improve those detention facilities, that is fantastic. A much bigger step would be to address the criminal justice system and its ability in countries like Nigeria and in East Africa to address processing of terrorism cases.

On the issue of political tensions, this is a very difficult one, and there are a number of different tensions. It is not just between the military and the State Department. Often there are different parts of the military that see this differently, I think. You might find that the regional commands view things differently sometimes than special operations commanders who are dealing with these countries on a more episodic basis.

But there are also political tensions between posts, the Embassy, be it both State Department and DoD officials and FBI officials, and others who have to manage those day-to-day operations, managing the relationship with the host country, and people back here in Washington, DC, who have to establish and implement the policies, including the Leahy laws. So there are tensions in terms of what your primary day job is, I guess.

And in terms of you mentioned Admiral McRaven's testimony last year, as I noted in my written testimony, he followed that up and said that there had been subsequently some very constructive engagement between DoD and the State Department.

And I think that as DoD has started to look more deeply at partner capacity-building, they are really having I think some constructive dialogues with the State Department on how to improve the process, improve the vetting process, improve the discussion with the host governments on how to hold forces accountable, how to provide this human rights training. So I think that that is moving in a positive direction.

Colonel AUBREY. Thank you, Mr. Chairman. I agree with Lauren about the ICRC. The only thing I would say, if—having dealt with the Nigerian Army, if they are putting it on their Web site, I assume it has the blessings from the highest level, and that means it is probably being checked.

As we all know, you know, soldiers do what they know that their officers are checking on. If they are taking it seriously, it is a positive movement forward.

Trafficking, I understand what you are saying. I know that any military member going into the SOUTHCOM area, one of the things that is required for entry is to complete—it is listed under force protection, but it really is training on human trafficking.

It is, once again, things that get checked, people do. If they are sitting down there—if that is a standard that becomes across the board, you will see a greater emphasis from the military. Obviously, in the SOUTHCOM area of responsibility, human trafficking had been a concern for the SOUTHCOM commander, and he acted accordingly.

INVEST—I understand the State Department has 13 people doing it. Mr. Rickard's number was 530,000 units checked. With one boss and 12 workers, that is a horrendous workload. I defer to Ms. Margon's bit about $5 million is much better than the $2 million. Obviously, it is a huge workload when you look at U.S. global engagement and having to validate a significant number of military units globally.

And the last comment on vetting, for that particular mission, we were able to reschedule. U.S. Army Africa has no dedicated forces to it. It is a headquarters. The Army's solution for that is to implement through—on the global manning process is to earmark what they call the regionally aligned force. And every year an Army brigade or a brigade equivalent is designated to the combatant commander to use for engagement opportunities.

There are finite periods. You know, that brigade commander or that unit commander has requirements that he or she has to meet. If they cannot deploy because the unit to be trained has not been vetted, it—you know, it will depend on what else the United States Army has earmarked for that unit the next quarter or the next fiscal year.

It might not ever recur. It could be an opportunity lost. It is very much dependent on the particular training being desired and when it is being scheduled.

Mr. SMITH. Colonel, before going to Ms. Massimino, did you find that the names that were tendered to you were more likely to be pre-cleared and to be of soldiers who are likely to make it, so in a way it is already having a laudatory effect on the Nigerian Army? And does it then begin to create a culture where human rights are the way forward for a soldier to really make it in the military, particularly if he is career-oriented?

Colonel AUBREY. The quality of U.S. training is superb. Most foreign nations—much broader than just Nigeria—select their best and brightest to come to the United States to go to our schools. So it is definitely a career enhancing move to be selected to come to the United States under the IMET program.

For training in theater, our soldiers are good. The quality of training that we give is good. Their soldiers benefit. So, yes, it would be a career-enhancing move to it.

As far as pre-clear on vetting, the Nigerians, when I was there, they understood what our requirements were. They knew far enough in advance because we were talking battalion level training, that we would check the names of every member of that battalion, and they had enough time to do it. And there was the political will at that time—and it was already addressed as—you know, then, peace support operations was very important to Abuja.

ASO Iraq did what was necessary and had the defense establishment do what was necessary to meet those terms. It is still, what is their political will to do so?

Mr. SMITH. Thank you.

Ms. Massimino?

Ms. MASSIMINO. Thank you. I don't have a lot to add to that. I want to also say that I don't know the content of the ICRC training for the Nigerian military, but I can't imagine that that is not a huge net plus, to have that happening. So it is good to hear that.

On trafficking, I am really glad you brought that up. I know that Leahy vetting sometimes includes things beyond what the law requires, but I would be also curious to know, and I don't know, whether engagement in trafficking by militaries is part of that.

I don't think I have had a chance to talk to you yet about the fact that Human Rights First is launching a major campaign on anti-trafficking efforts. And at a recent meeting with General Kelly, SOUTHCOM, at the human rights roundtable, we had a specific discussion about the concerns that criminal networks engaging in human trafficking are diversified and also are, you know, supporting terrorism, and it is becoming one large weapons, people, drugs, and terrorism network, profit network.

And so you could certainly make an argument that it ought to be, and I think we are going to be working closely with the U.S. military and others to try to ramp up efforts to identify those in foreign militaries that are engaging in trafficking.

And then, on the appeals process, Ms. Blanchard is far more knowledgeable about that than I am, but I did want to flag this, because it goes back to the importance of the duty to inform. Leahy really, again, to get the full benefit, it is not really going to work unless we are telling the people who are being excluded why they are being excluded, and then start working with them.

And I think there is sometimes a reluctance to do that, to make the relationship awkward, or we don't want to, or the governments aren't going to like it, and that has bled into sometimes kind of putting people in a strategic limbo where there is not a decision made. They don't want to make a negative decision, so they just put them in a closet and it never gets made. And that is not helpful either.

So those are things that it would be good to find some ways to tackle.

Ms. MARGON. Just very quickly, you know, I think on the $5 million, my response will speak both to the $5 million in the Senate appropriations bill and the tensions. What is very important to remember about Leahy is that there is both an Embassy side of this, so the U.S. Embassies are taking care of this, and there is the Washington side. That can breed tensions, not just along civ-mil lines, but also from posts back to Washington.

The $5 million, if you think about it, there is at least $15 billion of security assistance globally, the centerpiece of the President's counterterrorism plans as we redeploy from Afghanistan, is going to be this Counterterrorism Partnership Fund. Five million dollars to do the vetting is, assuming it is legislated correctly with Leahy requirements, we would hope, is that that is what needs to happen. It is a basic need to continue to expand the vetting pool that way.

So it would go to basic things like supporting staff and computers in Washington, but also enabling the Embassies, as I understand, to be better trained. It is desperately needed, and in the grand scheme it is not a lot of money to help move the process forward and make it easier, so when defense attaches at post have to do this vetting, it doesn't result in delays, it doesn't result in a misunderstanding, and names dropped off of people who should be.

The final thing that I would just mention is on the trafficking. As far as I understand, Leahy doesn't cover trafficking, since we are looking at just the gross human rights violations. But what I think it is important to note is that Leahy often works hand in glove with other conditions that have been put on through various bills, appropriations, and otherwise.

I think what we have seen in Indonesia and the Philippines is that Leahy has been the minimal basis along with some other conditions that have helped move those countries in the right direction. And so in considering next steps on trafficking, it may not mean Leahy has to change per se, but that there are additional alternative expansions that can be made and other bills that can work in a correlated way.

Mr. SMITH. Thank you. And just to add for your consideration, but I do think section 502(b) and the language clearly would cover trafficking. Look at the disappearance of persons, degrading treatment, cruel and inhuman, I mean, it is ready-made for that.

We will ask the administration, if they haven't, if they will include it, because it needs to be I think, and get the TIP office to weigh in as well, hopefully they will agree.

I do have one final question, and maybe—Ms. Blanchard, you answered it, but the Counterterrorism Partnership Fund, the $5 billion proposal which had legislative language—and I read the language and it right from your testimony, which came up on June 26, so just a few weeks ago—seems to not include the Leahy amendment.

I mean, with notwithstanding language red flags go up as soon as that language is anywhere, and it says notwithstanding any limitation in the provision of law that would otherwise restrict the amount or recipients of such support, does this bypass Leahy? Or am I misreading the language?

Ms. BLANCHARD. It could potentially, if enacted in that way. And the difficulty with these notwithstanding provisions, we don't always know how they are implemented. So it is not always clear when the administration makes a policy decision to use that notwithstanding authority or not.

But, yes, potentially that could, if that makes it into law, leave ways to—I don't want to use the term ''go around Leahy,'' but potentially.

If I could make one comment, CRS doesn't make policy recommendations, but on the issues of resources for vetting the new DoD definition of ''assistance,'' again, significantly broadens the amount of security assistance-type activities that the State Department will now have to be vetting for. And DoD is still, to my understanding, working on the definition of what all that includes, but it is significantly larger than the training that they were vetting for previously.

And if you then add on top of this the potential $5 billion new counterterrorism capacity-building program, that is a massive potential amount of vetting that needs to be done.

Ms. MASSIMINO. Yes. I just wanted to underscore that that is also in our recommendations about the $4 billion for the Counterterrorism Partnership Fund. And it is a huge red flag, and I think it is hard to understand that language in any other way. But Congress has an opportunity. You should not let that go past.

If there is, you know, any place where the Leahy vetting requirements should really be, you know, doubled down on, it is in this new strategy that the United States has for countering terrorism through these partnerships. That makes Leahy even more critical than it has ever been. And if this goes through with that notwithstanding language in it, it risks really gutting these important human rights laws.

Ms. MARGON. I would second that. It is a huge red flag for us, and very, very concerning. And it doesn't quite align with what the President said in his West Point speech. And if you look at the Syrian opposition, nobody in the administration talks about this new fund to go to the Syrian opposition unless they are talking about the vetted Syrian opposition.

And so the language that was sent up to Capitol Hill doesn't meet with the rhetoric that we have been hearing out of the administration, so it is very worrisome if it is implemented in that way.

Mr. SMITH. I do have one final question, because I did ask about INVEST. The Google search, INVEST—and thank you for your patience, especially with that very long voting that we had on the House floor, but—and then the input that comes in from NGOs and the human rights community, does the State Department, and DRL in particular, as well as the Embassies, have a sufficiently broad net to receive information from whistleblowers and people who— like a mayor who may know of something that needs to be told about what happened in his city, or an NGO that is indigenous in Nigeria, are we getting enough by way of a channel of information in that third part of the information flow?

Yes?

Ms. MARGON. I can talk about that a tiny bit, since we do a lot of the work. I think, again, it depends. It is case by case. It depends a lot on both the international and local organizations, the contacts that the officers have with the defense attache, and the political officers in the Embassy.

In the case of Nigeria, I think there is a lot of information flow. For Human Rights Watch, one of the things we have been trying to do a better job on when we do our research and reporting is be as clear as we can about the units that we observe and to get the information that will enhance Leahy vetting, whether it be the name we are told repeatedly from the State Department, date of birth, which obviously is very hard to get, but we try to include as much specific detailed information as we can to help that, and to pass that through both the Embassy channels and then back it up here in Washington.

And we work with some of the local organizations to do that as well, and we encourage the Embassy officers to reach out and to hold meetings in as much capacity as they can.

Mr. SMITH. Yes?

Ms. MASSIMINO. Again, I would just underscore that there are these human rights defender principles that, if they were fully implemented everywhere, there is nothing about them that specifically relates to Leahy, but it would in essence make it the practice of the U.S. Government to establish the kinds and depths of relationships with NGOs in these countries that would produce more detailed information that would make the Leahy vetting process work better.

Mr. SMITH. Yes. Ms. Blanchard?

Ms. BLANCHARD. One comment on the INVEST system. I think this online database is an incredible tool. You mentioned the issue of trafficking earlier. From my understanding, the State Department is trying to input a variety of other not necessarily gross human rights abuse related information, including on corruption and trafficking and other serious concerns on units when they have that information.

But then, of course, that goes back to the issue of time and resources to actually put that information into the system. So, again, going back to the 13 people staffing this at headquarters.

Mr. SMITH. I want to thank all of you for your extraordinarily incisive testimony, the expertise that you have brought to the subcommittee. This will be widely shared with my colleagues, and so thank you so very much, because I think it comes at a very, very important pivotal point.

And our hope is that more service members will be trained and trained to be effective, but also adequately and robustly vetted for human rights abuses, so that these troops are the kind of people we can be proud of, and Nigerians and others in other countries can be proud of.

I thank you, and the hearing is adjourned.

[Whereupon, at 5:12 p.m., the subcommittee was adjourned.]

APPENDIX

MATERIAL SUBMITTED FOR THE RECORD

SUBCOMMITTEE HEARING NOTICE
COMMITTEE ON FOREIGN AFFAIRS
U.S. HOUSE OF REPRESENTATIVES
WASHINGTON, DC 20515-6128

Subcommittee on Africa, Global Health, Global Human Rights, and International Organizations
Christopher H. Smith (R-NJ), Chairman

July 10, 2014

TO: MEMBERS OF THE COMMITTEE ON FOREIGN AFFAIRS

You are respectfully requested to attend an OPEN hearing of the Committee on Foreign Affairs, to be held by the Subcommittee on Africa, Global Health, Global Human Rights, and International Organizations in Room 2172 of the Rayburn House Office Building (and available live on the Committee website at www.foreignaffairs.house.gov):

DATE: Thursday, July 10, 2014

TIME: 2:00 p.m.

SUBJECT: Human Rights Vetting: Nigeria and Beyond

WITNESSES: Colonel Peter Aubrey, USA, Retired
                      President
                      Strategic Opportunities International

                      Ms. Lauren Ploch Blanchard
                      Specialist in African Affairs
                      Congressional Research Service

                      Ms. Elisa Massimino
                      President and Chief Executive Officer
                      Human Rights First

                      Mr. Stephen Rickard
                      Director
                      Washington Office
                      Open Society Foundations

                      Ms. Sarah Margon
                      Washington Director
                      Human Rights Watch

By Direction of the Chairman

COMMITTEE ON FOREIGN AFFAIRS

MINUTES OF SUBCOMMITTEE ON *Africa, Global Health, Global Human Rights, and International Organizations* HEARING

Day___*Thursday*___Date_____*July 10, 2014*_____Room_*2172 Rayburn HOB*_

Starting Time __*2:01 p.m.*__ Ending Time __*5:12 p.m.*__

Recesses |__*1*__| (*2:38* to *4:01*) (___to___) (___to___) (___to___) (___to___) (___to___)

Presiding Member(s)

Rep. Chris Smith

Check all of the following that apply:

Open Session ☑   Electronically Recorded (taped) ☑
Executive (closed) Session ☐   Stenographic Record ☑
Televised ☑

TITLE OF HEARING:

Human Rights Vetting: Nigeria and Beyond

SUBCOMMITTEE MEMBERS PRESENT:

Rep. David Cicilline, Rep. Karen Bass

NON-SUBCOMMITTEE MEMBERS PRESENT: *(Mark with an * if they are not members of full committee.)*

Rep. Robert Pittenger*

HEARING WITNESSES: Same as meeting notice attached? Yes ☑ No ☐
(If "no", please list below and include title, agency, department, or organization.)

STATEMENTS FOR THE RECORD: *(List any statements submitted for the record.)*

TIME SCHEDULED TO RECONVENE_____
or
TIME ADJOURNED __*5:12 p.m.*__

Gregory B. Simpkins
Subcommittee Staff Director